FOR ALL
Eternity

OTHER PRODUCTS BY
DR. JOHN L. LUND:

FOR ALL
Eternity

Dr. John L. Lund

Covenant Communications, Inc.

CONTENTS

FORGIVENESS

INTRODUCTION

"We just don't communicate!" How often have we heard someone say that? Or maybe we have said that about one of our significant relationships. Let's begin by suggesting that either you married your biggest communication test in life or you gave birth to it! Some of us will have both. Communication is at the heart of all relationships—husband-wife, father-son, mother-daughter, brother-sister, coworkers, or friends. Isn't it true that those we love most often present us with our greatest challenges? Communication is a vital part of any relationship. One of the things we talk about more frequently than anything else is how we fail to communicate with each other.

President Harold B. Lee is commonly quoted as saying, "Don't teach so they understand; teach so they cannot misunderstand" (see Tuttle, Theodore A., "Teaching the Word to the Rising Generation," 10 July 1970). That is a wonderful objective and a worthy goal, but how do we go from where we are to where we are communicating so clearly we are not misunderstood? One of the major objectives of this book is to help us understand what communication is and how we can use our improved communication skills to bring out the best in our relationships with others.

Frankly, most of us are quite self-centered, and we believe we are great communicators. It's the other person who has the problem of being a poor communicator. In order to understand what communication really is, we need to define it.

Communication is an exchange of understanding. It's an eternal truth that all frustration comes from unmet expectations. There is no such thing as someone who is frustrated who did not have an expectation that was unmet. If our expectation is to be understood, it becomes our responsibility as the speaker to accept ownership of our own words. This book will instruct us in how to achieve communication with understanding and to own our words. (You'll notice that several points in this book are repeated. I make no apology for that because the principles are explained in various contexts.)

Learning to communicate our expectations clearly requires skills that many of us have not learned in our unique and diverse family backgrounds. Even within the same family, different people have different ways of communicating with each other. Why? Because Mom and Dad came from different family backgrounds, and most of us are a hybrid of the communication patterns of our parents and siblings. People express acceptance, affection, and appreciation in different ways. Later in this book, we will explore how some people tend to be more verbal-, visual-, or touch-centered in their "love language" and in their general interactions with others.

In marriage education seminars, I often ask people, "How many of you feel you married into a weird family?" There is always a sea of hands raised, including my wife's hand, and, frankly, my own. The truth is that the families we marry into have developed their own styles of communication. Marriage and friendships bring us into a new world of how other people send and receive messages. We make a ton of assumptions about the messages we send and receive, and statistics tell us that about one out of every five messages is misunderstood, which often leads to arguments, hurt, heartache, and sorrow. The truth is, we are unique in our communication style as individuals, and it is our responsibility to accept that as fact. Until we do, we will transfer the responsibility for us to be understood onto the shoulders of others and lament their "poor communication."

Every marriage and every relationship struggles to develop a "common language" in which both parties are understood. Most of us define our friends by how well they understand and accept us. It is possible to stumble into a friendship where "understanding and acceptance" are obtained with little effort, but the reality of most of our significant relationships is that they require work and serious effort. Even when we are putting forth our best effort, we may find ourselves feeling hopeless or discouraged. However, it takes more than desire and effort to communicate. It requires new skills.

Years ago, Dr. John Gottman wrote a book entitled *Why Marriages Succeed or Fail* (New York: Simon & Shuster, 1994). After a twenty-year study with hundreds of couples, his research concluded that relationships fail because people lack willingness, knowledge, or skills. Obviously, the unwillingness of one or both parties in a relationship to learn new skills will result in frustration. The good news is that when one party develops new skills and knowledge of better communication techniques, the relationship changes. It has been said that insanity is repeating the same behavior over and over and expecting a different outcome. If we change our manner and style of communication with new knowledge and skills, we can improve all of our relationships. Remember, you have 100 percent control over 50 percent of the relationship. You control *your* half of the communications network.

I have had an active practice as a college professor, counselor, and marriage educator for more than forty years in the field of interpersonal communication. I can testify that when one party in a relationship develops new skills and knowledge, the dynamics of the relationship changes. As we accept the responsibility to improve our communication skills, we will find that we are less frustrated because more of our expectations will be met. This is not because the other people have changed, but because our ability to communicate our expectations in clear and kind ways has improved.

It is not easy to let go of the feeling that we should not have to change. If people love us, why can't they change to understand and communicate better with *us*? Imagine for a moment a group of English-speaking students traveling in Egypt. An Egyptian guide who does not speak English meets them. At first, the guide speaks to them in a normal tone of voice, but in Arabic. The students are frustrated; the guide is equally upset. Now the guide raises the tone of his voice to a scream. If people don't understand when you whisper in Arabic, will they understand if you shout in Arabic? This lesson applies to all our relationships. Husbands and wives often raise their voices thinking they will be more clearly understood when in reality they are speaking a foreign language in the first place. Just because two people speak English, Spanish, or Arabic does not alter the fact they came from different communication backgrounds and need to learn how to bridge the gap by sending and receiving messages in a common language.

All of us have come or will yet come to realize that communication is much more than *talking* or *listening*. People talk and listen all the time and never communicate. In their frustration, like the Egyptian guide, they raise their voices, believing it will make a difference. It doesn't. So let's define communication for what it ought to be: *Communication is an exchange of understanding.* If we have not had an exchange of understanding, we have not communicated, regardless of how much, how long, how intense, or how desperately we have talked and listened. One of our key objectives is to gain knowledge on how to improve our own ability to "exchange under-standing." At the same time, it is another thing to put this knowledge into practice. It takes time to develop skills. Just as bowling is a skill, so also is learning to communicate in a way that allows for an "exchange of under-standing." We are talking about changing our behaviors.

We will begin by recognizing that talking and listening are *tools* that may lead to improved communication. But they are only tools. Our objective is to develop the skills necessary to have an exchange of understanding. It only takes one person to change the dynamics of a relationship. You can be that person. I will make you a promise. If you will apply the principles explained in this book, you will become a more effective communicator, and more of your expectations will be met. If your expectations are not met, it will not be because you haven't communicated them clearly and with kindness. It will mean the other person is unwilling. Later in the book we will deal with how to negotiate with the unwilling, but first things first. Now let us begin by increasing our knowledge of men and women and learning how to "bridge the gender gap" of our communication differences.

Differences

CHAPTER ONE

Bridging the Gender Gap

Not only are there differences in how people communicate from family to family, but there are also major differences between the ways women and men communicate. The reality of male and female communication differences plays a significant role in our interactions. We tend to underplay these gender differences. Most women expect men to communicate like other women and most men expect women to communicate like men. It just isn't going to happen. Nor should it happen. There will always be exceptions to the rule. Not every man or every woman will fit neatly into these general statements about men and women. However, most will, and it will be useful for our general interaction to be aware of these differences.

The average man uses seven thousand communication signals per day. The average woman uses twenty-one thousand (see Pease, Alan and Barbara. *Why Men Don't Listen and Why Women Can't Read Maps*, New York: Broadway Books, 2001). Communication signals involve body language, facial expression, and tone of voice, as well as the words we use. The first difference between men and women is that, as evidenced by the statistics just mentioned, women use three times the communication signals that men use in a day. What does this tell us about men-women differences? It tells us that men use fewer words to transmit information and feelings than women do. This means that efficiency in using words is important to men. Depending upon the circumstances, there are three things most men want to know in a conversation:

1. Is this going to be painful?
2. How long is this going to take?
3. What do you want from me when this conversation is over?

I have counseled countless women to answer these three questions before they approach males of any age to see if the male response is not more positive. For example, a woman might say something like this:

"Honey, I would like to talk to you for two minutes, and it's not going to be painful." (Wait for a response.)

"Yes, what is it?"

"It would mean a lot to me if you would talk to our son, Greg. He's planning on going out tonight, and he hasn't finished his homework. Would you back me up and tell him he can't go until his homework is done?"

Without offending the entire female population, it is generally true that most women give men more information than men want to hear. It is not uncommon for the same woman to have approached her husband with the following information: "Honey, I need to talk to you about Greg. I talked to his teacher this afternoon, and she is a very conscientious teacher. She really cares about the students. She gives extra credit if the students are willing to help her work on special projects after school. Anyway, she called to express concern about Greg turning in his homework. She said he is doing well on the tests and in many ways is a model student. He participates in the class discussions. Anyway, I think Greg responds to you better than me and . . . and . . . and . . ." (the male brain has now checked out and is focusing on something else because he has no idea how long this is going to take or what she wants from him).

For most men this much is information overload. The average male, even if he patiently listens to the entire female explanation, would not be able to discern what he was expected to do as a result of all the information. In all probability, the woman would not get through this entire explanation without an impatient response from her husband, which might lead to an argument between the two of them that would not focus on the original issue at all, which is about Greg getting his homework done.

Because efficiency of words is important for men, they tend to become impatient and are prone to finish the sentence of the speaker, whether male or female, and they are inclined to interrupt. There is evidence that the male motivation and the female motivation for interrupting are different. Males are prone to interrupt because they are impatient, while women interrupt to add more information. Are there impatient women who interrupt and men who interrupt to add more information? Yes, but this particular generalization is given so that we might be aware of our different motivations for what appears to be the same behavior. This does not justify a man who is rude, insensitive, and constantly interrupting. He is wrong, and those are poor communication techniques. It also does not mean that men can't improve their listening skills.

It is equally true that most women want to *receive* more information than men are willing to share. As a general observation, women feel they have to pry information out of their husbands and male children. It is also customary for women to give lots of information and want to receive abundant detail, which males perceive as unnecessary. Most male conversations involve the transmission of information and very little, if any, feelings or emotions. One study of fathers communicating with their adult children indicated an average phone conversation lasted less than two minutes, while that same study showed that mothers' communication time with their adult children was quadruple and frequently involved thirty minutes or more.

Nurture or nature is a subject that has been debated for a hundred years in regards to males and females and their differences. Are men and women socialized to be a certain way? Yes. Are there genetic realities that incline us to certain behaviors? Yes. The historical pendulum has swung in both directions because both biology and socialization are important factors in determining behaviors. On one extreme, there was once a belief in the 1960s called *androgyny,* which held as its core belief that men and women were really the same except for the obvious biological differences. While such extremes are untrue, there is no question that socialization is a key factor in defining male and female roles in society. Therefore, women have the power to learn to be more effective communicators with men by analyzing the ways they've been socialized to communicate. They can ask themselves, "What is it I want this conversation to accomplish? What do I want from this man? Do I want to vent my frustration? Do I want my husband or son to do something? Am I looking for solutions or understanding?"

Understanding Versus Solutions

Here is another situation: My wife, Bonnie, will come to me frustrated with a problem. Sometimes she wants help with a solution, but most of the time, she wants understanding. Am I to become a mind reader, a body and facial expression reader? Am I to tune into universal karma? Perhaps if I tune in to her tone of voice, I'll be able to discern what she really wants—understanding or a solution. Maybe I am to actually listen to the words themselves to see if they will give me a clue.

How is a man to know whether a woman wants understanding or solutions? The answer is to say, "Honey, I don't know what you want from me. Do you want solutions or understanding, or do you need me just to listen while you talk? I'm serious because I really don't know."

It would be equally helpful if the woman said something like this: "I think for now I would like you just to listen and not offer any solutions. I want you to understand how frustrated I am, but I'm not looking for your opinion just now. You'll be my hero if you just listen to me for ten minutes."

Now, in our marriage, because I understand that Bonnie's expectations are different from my understanding of her expectations, I ask for a clear verbal signal as to exactly what she expects from me—understanding, solutions, or a listening ear. And Bonnie has learned to communicate more clearly. "Honey, on this one, I just need understanding." In my marriage, it boils down to one word. Bonnie can say, "understanding," or she can say, "solutions," and I instantly know what she wants from me. Now I have a better opportunity for success, and she's going to have less chance of becoming frustrated. The more precisely Bonnie can express her expectations, the greater the possibility those expectations are going to be met. The more nebulous or vague Bonnie is, the more she is setting me up for failure and herself up for frustration. This is true of all our expectations.

Men are brain-wired as problem-solvers, and so it's difficult for them to simply listen to women. When a woman says, "Oh, honey, I'm so frustrated. You know I did this and this." A man's natural reaction is to say, "Well, why don't you *do* this, why don't you *try* that? Let's just get to the bottom line and do this."

The woman counters with, "I don't want you to fix it, honey. I just want you to understand."

Without being properly prepared to give understanding instead of solutions, a man may respond out of frustration. He may say, "Well, then don't bring your problem to me if you don't want me to solve it."

This is why it's important for the woman to know what she wants from a man before she engages him in conversation. Generally, unless you tell a man differently, he's going to start giving a woman solutions as to how to fix her problems. If that is not what she wants, she needs to let him know.

Now, men can avoid frustration by asking, at the beginning of a conversation, "You know what, hon, I'm not sure whether you want understanding from me right now or if you want solutions." And women need to appreciate the fact that a man would be willing to ask that question. Often, women tend to think, "Well, if you really love me, you would know what I need. I shouldn't have to ask." We need to let go of that mind-set. We want people to understand our expectations without requiring them to be mind readers. Until we accept the responsibility to own our expectations clearly and kindly, we will live in the dysfunctional world of unrealistic and mostly unmet expectations.

The male propensity for economy of words suggests that once a man has used his seven thousand communication signals for the day, he is on overload. A lot of men wonder about this discrepancy between men and women and the difference in their communication styles. It is not unusual for men to feel deficient and inadequate about their inability to listen to long and involved female explanations. However, it's actually part of their biological makeup. But that doesn't mean men can't improve their listening skills. Some women I've talked with say they don't want my explanation of men's "economy of words" to be true because men will use it as an excuse for not giving more information. Some men may do just that. Other women have felt a sense of relief knowing that they and their husbands are normal.

After two years of post-doctoral research on the brain's wiring and the differences between men and women as it applies to communication, I've learned that our brains function differently. The scientific research on the female brain is relatively recent. Prior to 1982, most brain studies were conducted on dead soldiers. Studies since that time have disputed any claims of anatomical differences. However, using new techniques such as PET Scans (brain-mapping, in nontechnical language), we've discovered that there are significant differences in how men and women process information. But they are really quite simple. Men are monotaskers; women are multitaskers. Women can process several issues at once while males have a single-task orientation. This main difference affects the way males and females interact and communicate. It may help to explain why men are impatient with female information overload. The structure of the female and male brain is somewhat the same, but the actual processing of information is vastly different. Men and women think differently. To start with, the cells in a woman's brain are more compacted than a man's, and women have billions of neurons men don't have. These neurons are constantly sending information to the left and right sides of the brain.

As we know, the left and right sides of the brain have different functions but are connected by the corpus callosum. One of the foremost brain researchers, Dr. Reuben Gur of the University of Pennsylvania, reports that the corpus callosum is basically a pathway in the woods in the male brain as it relates to the transmission of information between the left and right sides of the brain. The female brain is a four-lane freeway. Some studies have reported that the corpus callosum is 30 percent larger in the female brain. This is amazing when one considers that the female brain is 11 percent smaller than the male brain. However, the female brain is more efficient in many ways. The best word that describes how the female brain functions is *integration.* Women are constantly integrating information. Even at night, only 10 percent of the female brain goes to sleep; 90 percent is sending messages back and forth and integrating that information. Contrast that with the male brain of which 70 percent goes to sleep at night and the other 30 percent is dedicated to snoring. I'm kidding about the snoring, but not about the 70 percent that goes into a state of rest.

Women tend to make connections with all the information they process, and they tend to integrate information in a process I call *personalization.* Personalization means women integrate information and internalize it. They apply the information to themselves. Here's how it works:

A woman and her husband are walking down the street, and the man looks over and sees a woman in a red dress. He says, "Oh, I like that red dress."

The woman may respond by thinking or saying, "Do you want me to wear a red dress? Do you like me in red? You think I ought to be wearing red?"

Stunned, the man replies, "No, I was just commenting on the red dress."

Men generally don't personalize information. Women constantly make statements to men that they hope men will internalize (personalize). A woman might say, "Doesn't that dark gray suit look good on that man?" She is hoping, of course, that he will think, "She's saying *I* would look good in a dark gray suit." But the man is thinking, "That's true; it does look good on that guy." He doesn't apply it to himself.

While women's brains are integrated, men's brains tend to be compartmentalized. Imagine the male brain as hundreds of compartments with doors going in and out of each compartment. Men tend to put information and feelings into compartments. For example, a husband and wife might have an argument at 6:00 PM, where cross words are spoken on both sides. A little later, each party apologizes. The male brain can put that experience into a compartment, close the door on it, and sleep like a baby. The integrating female brain may rehash this same experience days later as if the hurtful words have just been spoken. The male brain that put the argument away at 6:00 PM, turns amorous at about 10:00 PM, and invites the female to intimacy. In the male brain, the experience of 6:00 PM and the hurtful words are all locked up and sealed in a compartment on the left side of his brain. The typical female response is, "How can you even think about physical intimacy after what you said earlier tonight? And besides, on Mother's Day, you forgot to send flowers. Do you know how that makes me feel?" The female brain is integrating information from the past and present, while projecting that information and accompanying expectations into the future.

A major difference between brain function in males and females is that men can talk, think, and listen, but they tend to focus on one aspect of the three at a time. Women do all three at once. Research on male hearing indicates that men have a tonal range of five levels—the same as women. However, the male brain generally listens only to three tones. A crying baby down the hallway may be blocked out of the male listening range. A woman might say, "Can't you hear the baby crying?" Once it is drawn to his attention, the man says, "Oh, yeah," but prior to that, he may have turned down the volume switch in his brain, and the baby's crying was a part of "white noise." The female brain can also block out sound, but it still listens to all five tonal levels.

The same is true of all the senses. A man can be working on a car's engine and bloody his knuckles and not know it until someone points out he is bleeding. A man can be injured playing basketball and have a cut on his leg that he's not aware of until he showers later. This male biological trait of being a monotasker serves men well as protectors, warriors, and providers because it screens out nonessential "white noise" and allows them to focus on the task at hand. It doesn't make them very good husbands, however.

As multitaskers, women are biologically prepared to be great mothers. However, it can also create frustrated women if they expect men to see, hear, feel, and think as they do. Let's see if we can understand what it means that the male brain is monotasking. It means men can focus on talking, thinking, or listening, but when one has the primary focus, it means that dimmer switches are applied to the other two. If he is talking, he is not listening or thinking about other things. He is talking.

Men focus their vision in a primary range of about 45 degrees. If someone they are watching walks across the street, men will move their heads to keep the person in that 45-degree visual range. For example, if a pretty girl walks by, a man literally turns his head to watch her. Women also look at pretty girls and handsome guys but they only move their eyes. If both men and women look, why do women get so upset when men look? The answer is that men are so darn obvious about looking as indicated by their turning their heads. In addition, women are personalizing the information about his looking and comparing themselves to the woman. They are also questioning what his thoughts are about this other woman. Meanwhile, the male brain has put that woman in a mental compartment and moved on to think about sports and how his favorite team will fare in the upcoming game.

By the way, this whole process of men's and women's differences begins at conception, and somewhere between the fourth and fifth weeks after conception, we can start identifying maleness. A male fetus receives major infusions of androgens—one of which is testosterone—that will identify a fetus as male. These androgens affect the brain's wiring, and, by the end of gestation, the fetus has received five or six more rounds of androgens, sealing his maleness forever. By the time this process is finished, a male is going to be very compartmentalized and very much a monotasker.

Women, as multitaskers, can talk and think and listen all at the same time. Now, men are not so different that they can't walk and chew gum. But at the speed of electricity—about 93,000 miles per second—men will jump between talking, thinking, and listening, and even though men may feel like they're doing it all at once, they're not. Men are monotaskers who will talk *or* think *or* listen.

Often, when I'm thinking and my brain has turned down the dimmer switch on listening, I can hear Bonnie's voice in the background, but I'm not really listening. I hear an occasional word because I'm actually thinking. Bonnie will come up to me and touch me on the arm and say, "I've been talking to you for five minutes; you haven't heard a thing I've said." It's frustrating for her as a woman because she can talk and think and listen all at the same time. Another time she may ask me, "What do you think?" However, she does not give me time to think because she keeps right on talking, and I say, "I haven't had a chance to think yet. I've been listening. If you want me to think, I'll think. If you want me to listen, I'll listen, but I can't do both." This is foreign to the female brain. A woman can walk into a meeting where there are four or five women carrying on different conversations, and that woman can tune into *all* of those conversations. A man will walk in and think, "Why don't they be quiet and let one person talk at a time?"

Men Are Inherently Defensive

A major gender difference is the male's propensity for defensiveness. For thousands of years men have been warriors, and according to many psychologists, males are inherently defensive. This means *how* someone approaches a man will determine whether his response is defensive or cooperative. Edward T. Hall deals with this issue in a book entitled *The Silent Language* (New York: Anchor Books, 1973). Native Americans approaching one another would raise their right arm to the square as a peace signal. It was more than just a greeting. It also meant, "no weapon in my hand." Ancient Scottish men wore kilts and thigh-high stockings with a small dagger called a Sgian Dubh (pronounced "Skeen Doo"), at the top of the right stocking. Two Scots from different clans would approach each other at a safe distance and thrust their right legs forward exposing the handle of the Sgian Dubh still in its scabbard as a sign of peace. Studies show that men subconsciously look for exits when entering a new situation, whether that be a restaurant or a home or a new relationship. The point is men are inherently defensive.

It's helpful for women to realize this. Some women have come to this realization, but they don't know *why* the male is defensive. And men must be willing to admit they are defensive. I said to one man, "Do you know that you are inherently defensive?"

Before he thought about his response he said, "No, I'm not!"

I said, "Ladies and gentlemen of the jury, I rest my case!"

So, when a woman approaches a man, his first reaction tends to be defensive. "What do you want from me now? I am the guardian of my time. Do you want some of my time?" Remember earlier we said that there were three things men wanted to know when engaging in a conversation with a woman:

1. Is this going to be painful?
2. How long is this going to take?
3. What do you want from me when this conversation is over?

A number of women have said to me, "I think that for men to be defensive is silly. Why don't they just get over it and grow up?" Women who think this way are living on the wrong planet. What they are really saying is that men need to be more like women. That's true until you need men to be warriors. There are two kinds of warriors: defensive warriors and dead warriors. Good luck, ladies, expecting your men not to be defensive.

The idea that men are monotaskers is a good thing. It makes them good warrior-protectors and providers. Now, let me ask the women, Do you want your warrior-protector out there when he's sword-fighting and defending you to be thinking, "I wonder if my wife wants that small couch downstairs"? Those men aren't with us anymore. They're all dead. And if you saw the movie, *The Princess Bride*, they are not mostly dead, but dead dead. It serves the male gender well to be focused. But it is also true that men are capable of improvement and could work on being less defensive with the women in their lives.

Now, the other side of the issue is a woman's ability to be approached without being defensive. Women will evaluate the facial expressions and body language of someone approaching them and make a determination as to whether to be cautious, open, or defensive. The truth is, most women are not defensive unless they have been conditioned to react defensively by a critical husband or parent.

The Major Points of Men-Women Differences

Men and women process information differently.

1. Women use three times as many communication signals a day as men do.
2. Women tend to give men more information than men can process.
3. Men don't give women as much detailed information as women would like.
4. When a man is approached by anyone, he wants to know:

   a. Is this going to be painful?
   b. How long is this going to take?
   c. What do you want from me when this conversation is over?

5. The male brain is a monotasking brain, which means a man will focus on talking, thinking, or listening.
6. The female brain is a multitasking brain, which means a woman can talk, think, and listen all at the same time.
7. The male brain is highly compartmentalized. Information and feelings are placed in separate boxes, and men tend to focus on the present. Seventy percent of the male brain goes to sleep with all the day's information tucked into compartments for the night.
8. The female brain is highly integrated. Morning, noon, and night, the female brain is correlating information about all her relationships. Only 10 percent of the female brain goes to sleep at night. All night long she is thinking about the new information she has or doesn't have about relationships. (We know this because the PET scans show that the same parts of the brain that light up during the day when she is thinking about relationships also light up at night.)
9. Women personalize information. They apply it to themselves; men seldom do.
10. Men are inherently defensive.
11. As multitaskers, women come into their homes and are immediately aware of what's going on in all rooms of the house. The man is aware of the room he is in and where the exits are.
12. Women will have nine expectations for every one that a man has.

Applying This Information to Male and Female Conversations
For Women:
1. Let go of the expectation that men want to hear all the details you have to share.
2. Before you engage a male in conversation, ask yourself, "What do I want this conversation to accomplish? Am I looking for solutions or for understanding or do I just want to vent my frustrations?"

3. Men are inherently defensive, and how you approach them will determine whether they are defensive or cooperative.

For Men:
1. When you are not sure what your wife or daughter wants from you, be willing to say, "I'm not sure what you want from me. I don't know if you want understanding or solutions or if you just want to talk."
2. Work on not interrupting.
3. Give your wife or daughter a gift of love by just listening to them. Do not be impatient.

CHAPTER TWO

Say it Straight with Content Communication

Communication, in general, is a matter of interpreting meaning. We derive our meaning from three primary message systems. These involve

1. Facial expressions and body language
2. Tone of voice
3. The actual words themselves

I call the three of these together "Your Personal Message Filter."

According to Dennis Smith and L. Keith Williamson in *Interpersonal Communication* (Dubuque, Iowa: W.C. Brown Co., 1981), 55 percent of the weight we derive in understanding others comes from our reading their facial expressions and body language. Thirty-seven percent comes from listening to the tone of their voice. If we ask someone, "Will you please take out the garbage?" in a snippy way, he or she may respond, "Well, yes, but you don't have to be rude about it." To which we might respond, "I said please." But the word "please" is discounted because the tone of voice trumped our words. First, we read facial expression; second, tone of voice; and third, we give only 8 percent credibility to the actual words being spoken.

However, who is average? Who has an actual score of 55 percent, 37 percent, and 8 percent? What if your Personal Information Filter (PIF) gives 75 percent to facial expression and body language, 20 percent to tone of voice, and only 5 percent to the actual words? Your spouse, on the other hand, may give 25 percent to facial expression and body language, 25 percent to tone of voice, and 50 percent to words. Can you foresee a communication problem? Can you also see the need for a common language to which both parties can agree? There is such a language, and it is called content communication.

What is content communication? Instead of focusing on all three message systems, content communication focuses 100 percent on *words* as the primary system of communicating. It ignores facial expressions and body language; it ignores tone of voice. You hold yourself and the other person 100 percent accountable for the words used. You say what you mean and mean what you say, but you do it in a respectful way. Content communication is going to be the common language we agree to speak in which the listener can believe the speaker's words. Facial expressions, body language, and tone of voice are not a part of the equation.

Let's say you are asked, "Do you want to go with me to the store right now?"

Let's say you frown, you sigh, you shrug your shoulders, and say, "Yeah, I guess."

Content communication places 100 percent responsibility on our words. It ignores the frown and the shrug of the shoulders. It ignores the sigh. It holds us accountable for the words we speak. It assumes we mean what we say. "Yeah, I guess," is the same as "Wow, that's a great idea! Yes, yes. I really want to go with you to the store right now!"

As content communicators, you must own your words and your feelings. Remember, you are under obligation to say what you mean and to be held accountable for your words. If you are asked if you would like to go out for dinner and you say, "Yes," that means *yes*. If you have no opinion when asked where you would like to go for dinner, then say, "Anywhere," unless you *do* care. Because, as content communicators, you are responsible for your words. If you say that anywhere is fine, and then your spouse says, "Great, let's go have Mexican food," and you respond, "No, I don't want Mexican," it's too late. Your statement of "anywhere" has to mean *anywhere*. If you are willing to go anywhere except a Mexican restaurant, then you should have said, "Anywhere but Mexican." If you are uncertain about where you would like to eat, you might then say, "I'm not sure. Let's talk about alternatives, and I will react to the ones I like best." A statement to the effect of "I don't care" empowers the other person to make the choice.

Content communicating is a skill. It involves a speaker and a listener. The speaker speaks; the listener reflects back to the speaker his or her understanding of what the speaker is saying, and the speaker confirms that the listener does indeed understand. If the listener doesn't understand, it's the speaker's responsibility to send a clearer message. In other words, there are three steps to communication. Step one is the message sent by the speaker, or message-sender. Step two is where the listener reflects the essence of the message back to the sender. Step three is where the message-sender confirms that the listener has understood the message. Communication, the exchange of understanding, can be shortened to three words: speak, reflect, confirm. All three parts of the equation are essential. It takes practice, but it is the only way to overcome differences in gender and family background, and it helps us to navigate the quagmire of subtle meanings of body language, facial expression, and tonal messages.

Poor communication can be analyzed and understood. The first potential hazard rests with the speaker who does not send a clear message. Many speakers use confusing language, indirect messages, hint dropping, sarcasm, and any number of dysfunctional signals. Communicating clearly and in unmistakable terms rests with the message-sender. Poor communication and misunderstandings happen when the listener doesn't reflect the message to the message-sender. Generally both the message-sender and the listener are guilty of poor communication skills by assuming that an understanding has taken place. Only after step three has been successfully completed by the message-sender's confirming that the listener correctly understood the message has there been an exchange of understanding.

In using a combination of body language, tone of voice, and words, and in trying to interpret the true meaning of a message, we tend to misunderstand the message at least 20 percent of the time, and sometimes as much as 50 percent of the time. This means that one out of every five messages we send or receive is misunderstood.

On the job, this might mean that products show up at the wrong job site or that the wrong materials show up at the right job site. It means that money is wasted because messages have been misunderstood. The cost of one out of five messages being misunderstood is catastrophic to interpersonal relationships. "I thought that you thought that I thought . . ." is a common explanation for misunderstanding. But it seldom compensates for the arguments caused by the misunderstanding.

How many arguments involve "I thought you wanted . . ." or "I thought you meant . . ."? How much emotional blood is spilt every day in human relationships because of misunderstanding? How much hurt, heartache, and sorrow could be avoided if we truly understood each other? How many well-intended deeds have been dashed to the ground because they weren't understood in their proper context? How much mind-reading do we require from others in order to feel we are loved or valued? How much crying, pouting, depression, and human tragedy do we have to endure because we expect others to read our facial expressions and interpret them correctly?

When a husband and a wife become content communicators and place 100 percent responsibility on their words, they will only be misunderstood three out of every two hundred communications. That means by focusing on the words we use, we can decrease misunderstanding from forty out of two hundred to just three out of two hundred.

Where do the three misunderstandings come from as content communicators? Words mean different things to different people. This is known as semantics. Bonnie used to say things like, "Honey, *we* need to talk to our daughter" or "*We* need to take out the garbage." In regard to this last request, I envisioned Bonnie on one side of the garbage can and me on the other, and how *we* were going to take out the trash together. But you see, *we* did not mean *we*. *We* was *me*. Bonnie was diplomatically trying to get *me* to take out the trash. Alone.

Given enough time, men and women can pick up on these kinds of language quirks. However, there is a better way to communicate, and that is to say what you mean and mean what you say. Don't use *we* if you don't mean *we*. And ask for what you want in a kind way. "Dear, it would mean a lot to me if you would take out the garbage in the next hour."

And do *we* talk to our daughter about what it is *we* think we ought to be talking to her about? The answer is no, unless my wife clearly communicates the desired outcome of such a meeting. Otherwise, I'll have a great talk with my daughter, come out, and my wife will say, "Well, did you talk to her about this or that?"

"No."

"Did you talk to her about such and such?"

"No, but we had a great talk."

Content communicating is about stating the desired outcome clearly and with respect and kindness. Content communicating takes less effort, and it avoids the pitfalls of misreading body language, facial expression, and tone of voice. The greatest blessing of content communication is that it can be quickly implemented as it becomes our common language. Now, with content communication, it's important that our content, or our words, are delivered in a kind and respectful way. As content communicators, we do not have permission to be brutal or mean. We can say what we mean and mean what we say and be pleasant in doing so. It would be wonderful if the whole world would agree to be content communicators, but it won't. What this means is that we will still find those who expect us to correctly interpret all three message systems. But it's wonderful when husbands and wives agree to be content communicators.

A man who'd been married for fifteen years told me that his wife had asked him almost every night if he'd read his scriptures yet. This man was trying his hand at being a content communicator and said to her, "It kind of irritates me a little that you seem to have the need to check up on me every night to see whether or not I've read my scriptures."

His wife looked at him and said, "I don't care if you read your scriptures or not; I just want to know if I can turn out the light." Isn't that incredible? That is a great example of the very thing we're talking about—we tend to give indirect messages.

For most of us, it's difficult to shift to content communicating. We tend to come with a set of expectations based on our familial experience, where we're used to communicating a certain way and being understood a certain way. We tend to take these types of expectations and apply them to those outside our family circles. But it doesn't work that way. It isn't realistic. It may have worked in our family of origin, but it doesn't work outside of it. We may think that the other person needs to figure us out, and that if they really care about us, they will make the effort to figure us out. That's false thinking. It's unproductive, and it doesn't lead us to where we want to be. We want to be clear communicators. We talk about how we don't communicate in our marriages. One of the first things we need to focus on is communicating clearly so we can identify our needs and have a higher possibility of having our expectations met.

The challenge is for each one of us to become better content communicators. This will require us to hold both ourselves and others accountable for the words spoken. It becomes our common language. Of course, this is much more easily said than done. It's not easy to discount the other two message systems, to let go of reading body language, facial expression, and tone of voice. However, the rewards far outweigh the tradition.

When two people agree to become content communicators, to say what they mean and mean what they say and to do so in a kind way, life becomes sweet. There are no hidden agendas. You can trust the other person to ask for what he or she wants. There is no mind reading, no hint dropping, no test for true love, and no holding on to dysfunctional and unrealistic expectations. There is no setting someone up for failure and no setting yourself up for frustration. I counsel couples to assume only one thing—that their spouse is madly in love with them and that their spouse is pleased with everything they're doing. Be happy and know you are loved and valued, because if your spouse is unhappy with anything, it is his or her responsibility to come to you and own his or her frustrations so clearly that you cannot misunderstand.

CHAPTER THREE

Pitfalls

Even the so-called experts experience difficulty with accuracy in communication. To illustrate this point, I'd like to share my experience as a graduate student at the University of Washington, where I studied interaction analysis in depth with some of the best in the field. For all our dedication, study, and expertise, when it came to our ability to interpret someone else's communication, we experts were wrong 20 percent of the time! Having taken classes in reading body language and facial expression, we thought we were prepared to decipher just about any communication style. But in an experiment in interaction analysis, we were asked to place a person in one of ten communication categories every three seconds based on their communication style. Even with our experience, and even with all the analyzing and graphing and charting, we were wrong 20 percent of the time.

One of the most important things we learned was that there are communication pitfalls.

Mixed Messages

Are all three message systems always congruent? No! Do our facial expressions and body language, our tone of voice, and our words all consistently send the same message? The answer is not always. Many times our face says something different than our words do. This is called a "mixed message."

A boss enters the office with an intense look on his face, and he is pacing the floor. You ask, "Are you okay?"

He answers gruffly, "Yes, I'm fine."

Do you believe him? No. Because in sorting out the message, you give greater credibility to his facial expression and body language than you give his tone of voice or choice of words. In this case, you correctly interpret the mixed message, but you don't know why he is upset. Maybe he just forgot his keys. Maybe he needs to go the bathroom but someone is already in there.

The dilemma is in interpreting all three message systems correctly. When people are negative and their facial expression, body language, tone of voice, and words are congruent, we know they are upset, but we may not know why unless they are willing to own it and let us know. Moreover, we're easiest to read when we're in the negative, but often, the stated reason is not the real reason. For example, a man may yell in anger at one of his children for leaving the bike in the driveway when the real reason he's upset is because he backed into a pole and broke a taillight on the car at the job site. The truth is, he's upset with himself, but he transposes a disproportional amount of his anger to the child for leaving his bike in the driveway. It's not easy to know what the true issue is.

We do our least effective communicating when we send mixed messages. People are not sure what the message is. Remember, remember, remember, it is the responsibility of the speaker to communicate clearly their expectations of others and to do it in a kind way.

I remember early in our marriage asking Bonnie, "Honey, would you like to go to a late-night movie?"

Bonnie frowned and responded unenthusiastically, "Yeah."

What was that?

The tone of Bonnie's response indicated to me that she didn't want to go even though her words said yes. What she meant was, "Yes, I'll go, because if I don't you are going to be a big baby and pout." I read the facial expression as a no. I read the tone of voice as a no, but her words said yes. So, according to the formula, 92 percent of the credibility of her answer (as based on facial expression of 55 percent and tone of voice 37 percent) went to no. Eight percent (as based on the actual verbal answer) went toward her yes answer. Can you see how difficult it is to truly achieve an understanding?

If You Have to Ask, It Does Count

I once encountered a situation where a family had five different divorces going on at once—five siblings involved in this crisis of divorce. One of the family members said, "Maybe it's our family's style of communicating; maybe that's a problem." So they invited me to do an analysis of their communicating. I interviewed all five couples as well as the mom and dad. I was invited for Sunday dinner. As they ate dinner, I watched their interactions. And as I watched everyone interacting, one of the things that stood out was the fact that when the father of these five siblings wanted something, he didn't ask for it. He stared at it. The father was sitting at the dinner table, and he began to stare at the peas. I thought, *Is this a prelude to a heart attack? What's going to happen with this guy?* He continued to stare, and pretty soon somebody noticed and said, "Dad, would you care for some gravy?" The gravy was right next to the peas. He shook his head and kept staring. Finally, somebody handed him the peas, and he smiled.

Later, I was sitting on the couch with the dad, and I said, "Let me ask you a question. Don't be offended by this, but I just really want to know. Why didn't you *ask* for the peas?" His response was, "If you have to ask, it doesn't mean as much."

How many of us are holding on to the same dysfunctional thinking—"If you have to ask, it doesn't count?" Later, I met again with all five couples and confronted them with owning their expectations clearly and in a kind way. Four out of the five siblings would not let go of the expectation that you shouldn't have to ask. All four relationships ended in divorce. The one sister who said she was willing to change and to own her expectations clearly and in a kind way stayed married. A footnote to that story is a comment from her husband, whom I encountered at a Wal-Mart about six months later. He said, "I can't thank you enough. For the first time in our marriage of eight years, I feel I can be successful and meet my wife's expectations. I honestly never knew what she wanted before, and she wouldn't tell me because, as you said, she had grown up with 'If you have to ask, it doesn't mean as much.' I love her and always have, but I was tired of constantly being a disappointment to her. Now when she slips into that old habit, I just say, 'Dr. Lund.' She immediately responds. It was her willingness to change her dysfunctional expectation that has saved our marriage."

Too many people are prone to think, "If you really care, you will become a mind reader." This comes across as either naïve, narcissistic, or overwhelmingly self-centered until we realize that others do not process information the same way we do.

I watched my mother, her three sisters, and my grandmother prepare a lunch for a birthday party without saying a word to each other, and I remember asking them, "How did you ladies do that?" My mother said, "You have eyes, you know. All you have to do is open your eyes and look at what needs to be done." What happened with these women was that one of them would look and say in their own mind, *Is anyone setting the table? No, I will go and set the table.* And so they prepared lunch without what I would call traditional communication. Within the family of origin, everything was clear.

All this was based on anticipating the needs of the others and meeting those needs before they were requested. All five of these ladies lived their lives anticipating the needs of others and meeting those needs without having to be asked. Because that is how they showed love and concern, they expected others to respond in a similar manner. I know for a fact that none of my uncles, or my father, or my grandfather ever got it. To the credit of my mother and a couple of her sisters, they learned to improve but never fully let go of the expectation that it always meant more when you didn't have to ask. I disagree. It means everything when the people we love respond to our needs when asked to do so. To believe otherwise assumes that mind reading is a virtue when it is not.

Don't Ask If You Don't Want to Know

It is better not to ask a male his opinion unless you really want his opinion. For example, Bonnie asked, "Do you think we ought to paint the upstairs bathroom?" She was hoping, of course, that I would say, "Yes, the bathroom looks a little dingy, and painting it would make it look nicer."

As a content communicator she should say, "I want to paint the upstairs bathroom. Would you help me with that project on Saturday morning for an hour and a half?" Some women may find this hard to believe, but most men want to please their wives, and when approached with a request, will respond in the positive most of the time. If, however, she approaches him with twenty tasks, she may find him reluctant.

It is a mistake to ask a male for his opinion and then argue with him if his opinion does not agree with yours. Once a male has formed an opinion, it is his defensive nature that will cause him to defend his opinion to the death. Well, maybe not to the death, but certainly to verbal conflict. Why would any woman want to set herself up for conflict by asking a male his opinion if she already has an expectation she would like implemented? Once you ask a man what he thinks and he formulates an opinion that is contrary to your expected outcome, you have added a new barrier to your objective. Few things upset men more than being asked for their opinion and having that opinion rejected or torn apart in favor of another opinion. Men are known to defend their opinion even if it's not the best, because what they are defending is their ego and their feelings of self-worth. All of this unnecessary conflict could be avoided with content communication, by just asking for what you want in a kind and pleasant way.

Another content communication approach would be to ask for an opinion by laying the proper groundwork: "Hon, I'm considering which project I might take on next. I want your opinion, but I would also like you not to feel hurt or rejected if I consider your opinion and choose something else. Would you be willing to give me your opinion as one option, because I really would like to know how you feel? However, I am also asking you to support me with whatever choice I make after considering all my options."

Asking Leading Questions

Asking leading questions often involves asking someone's opinion when you really don't want it. Some people will ask a question hoping that the other person will respond in a way consistent to the speaker's unspoken expectations. For example, if I want a milkshake, I should not ask Bonnie, "Would you like to stop and get a milkshake?" My hope, of course, is that she will say, "Yes, let's stop and get a milkshake." Instead, she says, "No, thank you, I would rather go directly home." Now I have a problem. That is not the answer I was looking for. Now I have to overcome her request to go directly home. My "leading question" has now set up a conflict between going directly home and getting a milkshake.

So I ask her a second, third, or fourth time, "Are you *sure* you don't want a milkshake?" By the third or fourth request, she will be upset because her stated opinion was that she would rather go directly home. The appropriate content communication statement would be, "I would like to stop for a milkshake before we go home. Would you like one?"

If Bonnie really needs to get home and doesn't feel there is time to stop, her response should be, "It would really mean a lot to me if you take me straight home and then came back for a milkshake." That is content communication. For Bonnie to agree to stop for a milkshake that would make her late for another appointment would cause her to be resentful. I'm quite certain that the milkshake is not worth the resentment, and if a milkshake is truly that important to me, I need to own my expectation and get a milkshake after dropping her off.

Once you have practiced content communication for a while, you will find that you don't need to ask the same question more than once.

"Would you like to go out for dinner?"

"No, I don't think so."

"Are you sure?"

That is not content communicating. In content communication you don't need to ask the same question more than once.

Hint Dropping

Another form of communication that causes potential grief is hint dropping. This is another communication dysfunction. About 80 percent of us come from hint-dropping families. I'm going to confess right now that I come from the queen of hint droppers. I came into marriage with a myriad of hint-dropping skills, and the measure of my wife's love for me would be, of course, whether she could pick up on these hints.

Let's look at an example of what I mean by hint dropping. My mother wanted the kitchen garbage taken out. I was sitting in our family room, and my dad was in the kitchen with my mother. As I was watching television, I heard my mother start to sniff the air. I remember thinking to myself, *She wants the garbage taken out.* Isn't that amazing? How did I know her sniffing meant, "Take the garbage out"? She is my mother, and I was raised with a course in upper-division "Sniffology." There were different kinds of sniffs. A long, drawn-out sniff meant, "You stink and need to take a shower." But three short sniffs meant the garbage was stinking and needed to be taken out. Now, my dad came from the old school, where real men kept white, ironed hankies in their back pockets. When my mom started sniffing, of course, Dad reached into his back pocket and offered her the hankie. She put her hands on her hips and said, "No," visibly irritated that he hadn't picked up on clue number one. *If he really cared, he would . . .*

Dad was baffled, and I was chuckling. I was thinking, *He doesn't get it. She wants the garbage taken out.* I didn't say that, by the way—I wouldn't say that to my dad. But I thought it. And I didn't look over toward them because if I looked, I would have to take the garbage out. That was another nonverbal communication thing. So I didn't look. I just listened. And I could hear the disgust in Mom's voice.

Then I heard clue number two:

"Can't you smell it?" *Sniff, sniff.*

"No, hon. Smell what?" my dad said. Of course, I believe my dad couldn't smell a dead skunk in front of him, but he gave a couple of sniffs anyway.

Now Mom was really frustrated. Two very profound clues and Dad hadn't gotten either one. See, you get full credit if you get it on the first two clues, but if you have to give three clues, you don't get full credit anymore. So now, even if he did get it and take out the garbage, he would not get full credit. He had missed his opportunity. Mom's third and final clue was to stare at the garbage, which, by the way, was under the kitchen sink behind two doors. Dad followed her stare, which was fixated on the kitchen sink, looked at her in utter amazement, and said, "You want the garbage out!" Of course, Mom was disgusted and probably exhausted. This kind of communication takes a lot of energy.

In her family of origin, had she started sniffing, her mother and three sisters would have immediately begun to look for a dirty diaper. Well, since Dad had finally gotten it right, Mom answered, "Yes!" She sighed deeply and added, "Do I have to draw you a picture?"

My father rolled his eyes and noticed me. In a very loud and determined voice, he said, "Okay, son, get in here and get that garbage out. And

I mean now!" I knew I would be taking the garbage out the moment Mom started sniffing. So I took the garbage out.

When I say my mother is the queen of hint droppers, she really is, and I love her. She's eighty-seven years old now, and I don't think she's going to change, but I have.

Let's talk about a couple who'd been married for quite some time. In visiting with this couple, I said, "Well, you folks have been together for a while. How long have you two been married?"

She answered, "Fifty-one years; we've been married fifty-one years."

I said, "Whoa, that's good."

He said, "No, we haven't."

They had a problem.

He went on to say, "You know, I don't know anything more about her now than I did one year after we were married. We've been married one year, fifty-one times."

I looked at him, and he said, "You ever seen a wet chicken?"

I replied, "Well, yeah, I've seen a wet chicken; I was raised on a farm. I know what a wet chicken looks like."

"You ever seen how they plump out their feathers?"

"Well, yes. I've seen chickens fluff their feathers."

"Well, that's what she does," he responded. "I don't know what I've done to get her upset, but I know when she's fluffing and gawking at me that I've done something wrong. When I ask her what's wrong, she says, 'You know, but you're too stubborn to do anything about it.'"

As a counselor, I asked her, "What is the problem as you see it?"

"The problem is that he's insensitive. He's always been insensitive."

What did she mean by that? What she meant was, "He didn't grow up the way I grew up. And because he didn't, he's guilty. See, *I* grew up the right way, and he obviously doesn't love me. He doesn't really care, because if he did, he would respond to my requests."

I asked her to give me an example.

She said, "Well, we were driving down the road. I looked right at him and said, 'Dear, it's very hot,' and he looked back at me and said, 'It really is,' and kept right on driving."

Now, how many of us know what she wanted? The ones who know are hint droppers. I would like to welcome you to Hint Droppers Anonymous. Statistically, about 80 percent of hint droppers come from hint-dropping families. However, different families have different hint-dropping styles. So even if one hint dropper marries another hint dropper, they may not understand each other's hint dropping.

I said to the guy, "Well, what were you thinking?"

He said, "I was thinking, *You're right; it really is hot.*"

"Well, didn't that trigger something in your mind that maybe she wanted something?" I asked.

He said, "No, it was hot, and I agreed with her."

I looked over at his wife, and she was fluffing, gawking, and sighing. Fifty-one years of two wonderful people enduring so much unnecessary hurt, heartache, and rejection when owning their expectations clearly and in a kind way would have solved their problem.

The story goes on. Back in the car, the husband asked her, "What did I do wrong now?"

She said, "I asked you to turn on the air conditioning."

"No, you didn't. You said it was hot, and I agreed with you."

She retorted, "Do I have to draw you a picture?" (It was like a voice from my past.)

"One year of marriage fifty-one times," the man explained.

She said, "That wasn't the end of it."

"It wasn't?" I asked.

"No," she answered.

"What happened?"

"Well, he turned on the air conditioning, but a couple minutes later I looked up and saw this 7-11 about a block and a half away. I looked right at it. Then I looked at him, looked back at the 7-11, and said as clearly as I could, 'Dear, I'm very thirsty.'"

So I asked the husband, "What did you think when she said that?"

"I thought she was very thirsty," he observed.

"What did you do about that thought?"

"I thought, *We're about four minutes from the house; I'm going to put the pedal to the metal and get this woman home and get her something to drink.*"

So he blew by the 7-11 at about seventy miles per hour.

And she was as mad as a wet hen and immediately began to fluff and gawk.

He looked over at her. "What's wrong now?"

Fifty-one years of that.

It was at this point that I promised her an end to this problem, but I explained that she would have to learn to communicate her expectations so clearly they could not be misunderstood and to do it in a kind way. She was reluctant to accept responsibility for the fact that she was a poor communicator of her expectations. The truth is, she was shocked that I thought she was the problem. As a retired English teacher, she understood that a declarative statement was not an interrogative. To say "It's very hot" is to make a declaration. It's not a request for behavioral change. To say "The earth is filled with war," is a declarative statement. Does that mean you have requested that I go out and establish world peace? I asked her to stop expecting declarations to mean something they didn't. I told her, "In the future I want you to say, 'It's really hot. Would you please turn on the air conditioner?'"

It took six sessions to get her to agree to be a content communicator, to be able to state her expectations clearly. It wasn't easy. She assumed that she shouldn't have to be that explicit. She thought we should be able to give others a general hint and, if they really cared, they would learn to understand. It's kind of like the girl who drops a hankie because she wants a man's attention, and if he picks up the hankie, she knows he's interested. There is too much hurt, heartache, and sorrow in that kind of communication. So, finally, after the sixth session, here's the way that she learned to communicate. I said, "You are driving down the street, same scenario. What are you going to do?"

She said she would say, "Dear, it would mean a lot to me if you could turn on the air conditioning. I'm very hot," and "There's a 7-11 about a block and a half away, and I am very thirsty; I would like you to stop and get me a 44 oz. Big Gulp Sprite."

This is content communicating. This couple learned a new skill, and it changed their lives. I will never forget what the husband said to me later on. "Where were you fifty-one years ago? We have gone through so much heartache with her believing I didn't love her and didn't care when the truth is, I do love her, and I do care. But I've never been able to pick up on what it was that she really wanted from me. I couldn't find a label for it or identify it like you did. But this means everything. These last couples of months have been the best months of our marriage. I finally feel like I can be successful in this relationship. I don't mind turning on the air conditioning. I don't mind opening doors and doing all the things she would like me to do. I'd felt like I was condemned because I couldn't figure it out. And because I didn't think the way she thought and the way her family thought, she'd made the assumption that I didn't care, when the truth is, I care very deeply."

It's quite evident how challenging both hint dropping and If-you-have-to-ask-it-doesn't-mean-as-much can be. These are two dysfunctional communication patterns that are blind spots for most people. They represent an unrealistic expectation that if someone loves you, he or she will eventually get it. Few ever do, and most never figure it out—even if they have been married for fifty years.

Our good communication skills and our bad ones were learned before the age of eight and were reinforced up to age twelve. The Bible says "train up a child in the way he should go: and when he is old, he will not depart from it" (Proverbs 22:6). It is hard to let go of our early childhood training even if our expectations are dysfunctional. What does dysfunctional mean? It doesn't function. It means it doesn't work. Learning replacement behaviors and putting them into practice is hard but it is the only healthy solution. The thing that we can do as a communicator is to focus on clearly delivering a message of what our expectations are. It makes us a more effective communicator. Conversely, anything we do to take the focus off the message is going to make us less effective as a communicator. If we really want to be effective, we will want to eliminate these hint-dropping behaviors and mind-reading expectations. It's important for a healthy relationship to find ways to communicate clearly and in a kind manner.

Do You Really Want to Be Surprised?

I can't tell you the number of gifts my wife has taken back. So I would rather she give me a list of four or five things she wants and where to buy them. Then she can be surprised at the one I come back with, and she can buy the other four for herself. It's better for her to give me a list than for me to try to tune into her hints and surprise her.

One time I surprised her. I gave her a blue and avocado-green couch. It stood out when I saw it at the store; that's why I got it. I thought, *Boy, this is really going to impress her.* See, in my heart and soul I liked to surprise her. She was surprised. She suggested we call our interior decorator friend and ask her opinion on how the couch would look in our front room. Our front room was in autumn colors, by the way.

Our decorator friend came into the room, and the couch just about knocked her over.

I said, "Doesn't that stand out?"

She said, "It really does. Take it back."

It was easier to hear it from her than from my wife. "You don't want it to stand out. You want it to kind of blend in. This stands out. When you come into the room you don't even know there are walls in this house because all you see is a blue and avocado-green couch leaping at you," she said. "You can keep the couch if you want to, but you are going to have to spend several thousand dollars on new carpet, wall coverings, and a new decor to go with it." It didn't take me long to make the decision to take it back. Bonnie was greatly relieved that this interior designer, whom I had great respect for, advised me to take it back.

So, how do we surprise someone? I'm not so sure we want to. Not with a blue and avocado-green couch. With the number of dresses I've bought my wife, I'm always thinking she'll really like this dress, but finally she said, "Honey, I've been color coded, and if you are going to buy me something, here are some swatches."

If a woman really wants to be surprised, she'd better be gracious about whatever she gets. If she doesn't really want to be surprised, it would be better she content communicate and give her man at least two or three possibilities. "Here are two or three things that would be wonderful; I would love any of them." She could even give him a list of where he could go to get them. Women must be very clear about that, and then be happily surprised at which one on the list he brings back.

As mentioned in the introduction, all frustration comes from unmet expectations. There's no such thing as somebody who's frustrated and doesn't have an unmet expectation. Now, the question is, are our expectations well communicated? Our natural tendency is to think, "I don't have a problem; no one has a problem understanding me." This may be true when it comes to our family of origin understanding us. We may not have a problem communicating with those we've known from our youth where our language skills were developed or with some friends who came from a similar communication background. But when we marry someone from a different family, this is no longer true. And so, once again, "We need to learn how to communicate not only so clearly that we are understood, but so clearly that we are not *misun-*derstood" (Harold B. Lee). This means our expectations must be clearly defined. If we want to be understood, we need to let the other person know it. Assumption is the mother of misunderstanding. Remember, one out of five of all our communications is misunderstood. In some relationships, more than half of all communications are misunderstood. Why would anyone want to be a poor communicator when owning their expectations clearly and with kindness is easier in the long run?

The thing that makes content communicating such a wonderful principle for me is that I don't have to worry about what Bonnie is thinking, what is going on in her mind. I don't have to wonder if she's upset about this or that. A person can carry on an entire mental debate about what they think is happening in another's persons mind only to find that it wasn't reality at all. Why would we fabricate heartache and sorrow when there's already enough to go around?

CHAPTER FOUR

A Relationship of Equals

Marriage is a relationship of equals. No one brings his or her mate to the marriage altar in a headlock and preemptively demands he or she says yes to the marriage. It was common consent that brought the couple to the marriage and common consent should be the governing principle that sustains the marriage. When the Lord married Adam and Eve, He said, "And they shall be one flesh" (Genesis 2:24). Oneness has to do with unity. It doesn't necessarily mean we feel the same way about everything. It means we come to an agreement, which may be less than either of us wants but a decision we will both support with a good attitude. "Be one; and if ye are not one ye are not mine" (D&C 38:27). Unity is more important than "getting your way."

What if we're a very clear content communicator and the other person refuses to be? Now that we've talked about being clear in our communication, the second issue may be that we have to negotiate for what we want in a relationship of equals. If there is something about which you feel strongly, and your spouse is unwilling to support your request, ask the following question: "What is something I could do for you that would compensate for this thing I would like you to do for me?" In a relationship of equals such as marriage, compromise and negotiation are expected realities. One is never required to compromise if something is illegal or immoral. Painting the bathroom or not painting the bathroom, going to Disneyland or not going to Disneyland, is neither illegal nor immoral, but it may be an important personal desire.

"Does everything have to be a negotiation? Why can't my spouse just do what I want them to because he or she loves me?" Some couples have to negotiate more than others, but all marriages involve compromise, sacrifice, and negotiation. There are generally two reasons people are not motivated to do things for their spouse. One is they feel an imbalance of power, coercion, or resentment. The second reason, and the most common one, is they feel unappreciated for the contribution they are already making. They lack motivation. That is why this question is so powerful: "What is something I could do for you that would compensate for this thing I would like you to do for me?" It addresses the issue of motivation. It shows a willingness to be in a relationship of equals.

A husband-wife relationship as a relationship of equals means that you are not my parent, and I'm not your parent. In a relationship of husband and wife, we are coworkers with equal authority. The proclamation on the family talks about the husband and wife being in a relationship of equals: "In these sacred responsibilities, fathers and mothers are obligated to help one another as equal partners" ("The Family: A Proclamation to the World," *Ensign*, Nov. 1995, 102). President Hinckley, in talking about 1 Corinthians 11:11, said, "Under the gospel plan marriage is a companionship, with equality between the partners" (*Teachings of Gordon B. Hinckley*, Salt Lake City: Deseret Book, 1997, 322). It is an expansion of "neither is the man without the woman, neither the woman without the man, in the Lord" (1 Corinthians 11:11). If one partner has a request to make, he or she will do it respectfully, and the couple will then talk about it together. There can be no coercion, no manipulation, and no unrighteous dominion.

In order to be able to negotiate, we must learn to speak the language of equals. Language is appropriate to stewardship, and there are three basic stewardships in society. There is the parent figure; in employment circles we call this a boss. There is a language that is consistent with a boss or parent. That language is called *directive* language. It is totally appropriate for a boss or parent to use directive language: "You should," "You need," "You ought." *Should, need,* and *ought* are terms consistent with boss language. However, directive language is totally inappropriate for the husband-wife relationship. It's like telling the prophet what he should, need, or ought to do. And yet in many of the husband-wife relationships I'm familiar with, partners simply take turns parenting each other, telling each other what they should, need, or ought to do. When we think we are right on whatever issue, we feel it somehow authorizes us to parent our partner. It doesn't.

The language of a child is what we call *permission* language. Permission language is the "May I," "Can I," kind of language, and that language is not appropriate for a husband-wife relationship either. The husband-wife relationship is a relationship of equals, and the language of equals is the language of respect and request. It sounds like this: "It would mean a lot to me if . . ." "Would you . . . " "Could you . . ." "I would appreciate it if . . ."

For example, if I have something critical I want to say to Bonnie, she's my equal. I'm not her father. I'm not her child. Because we are in a relationship of equals, if I am going to communicate a criticism to her, I might approach it like this: "Bonnie, I have something critical I want to share with you. When would be a good time to do it?" And she might say, "Well, not now. I'm getting ready for my little group of Primary activity day girls."

"Well, my comment is about the Primary girls."

Bonnie responded, "Okay, what is it?"

"The last time you and the girls were together you made sixty cupcakes, and it was a disaster. The house was a mess when you were done, and I wound up cleaning it up. Could you make it a part of your projects to leave time for clean up? It would mean a lot to me. I'm glad you're helping these eleven-year-old girls, and I admire your commitment. If it's too late today, I'll understand, but maybe for future meetings you could consider it."

As equal partners, we must ask ourselves whether we speak the language of request and respect or whether we parent one another: "You should be home at this time," and "You should be doing this," and "You should be taking out the garbage," and "You need . . . you should . . . you ought." If someone followed us around with a tape recorder and listened to our conversations, what would it reveal about the nature of our interactions? Do we treat one another as equals? We must practice owning our words, saying what we mean and meaning what we say, not in a brutal or an unkind way, but with respect and request and as equals.

One of the things Dr. John Gottman pointed out that really made an impression on me was this: How we approach a person may very well determine the outcome of our interactions independent of the merits of the situation. Basically what this means is that if Bonnie approaches me as a mother figure with language like, "You ought to be doing this," and "You ought to be doing that," it doesn't matter what she's saying; her approach has destroyed my ability to focus on the content of her message because I feel like I'm being parented—being told what I should, need, and ought to do.

Now, in a perfect world, I would be able to sort through all of that and look at the message behind the approach. Unfortunately, we don't live in a perfect world. And it's a self-defeating behavior to approach an equal as a parent. So if I want to share something with Bonnie, or if I want something from her, I need to first ask myself, "Am I coming across as a parent, a child, or an equal?"

Introvert Versus Extrovert

Another important aspect of establishing a relationship of equals is understanding what types of things are motivational to different types of people. How do men and women recharge their batteries? It may be different betweens spouses, and it helps to understand a little about the differences between introverts and extroverts. There tends to be some misunderstanding about these terms. I have found the following definitions helpful. An introvert is *not* someone who doesn't have good social skills. An introvert is a person who needs a certain amount of alone time in order to recharge their batteries. That's how we define introversion. Actually, the top sales people and top socializers are often introverts. Social interaction, however, drains the introvert. Some introverts possess great social skills, but those skills do not charge their batteries. So when they come home, they want to be alone. They want to sit down in front of a television or computer screen and simply stare at it. If the wife says, "Honey, that's the microwave," and the introverted husband answers, "Yeah, but I like what's on," he may need a certain amount of alone time.

Now, if a husband or wife is an extrovert, he or she may need a certain amount of social interaction. For extroverts, too much alone time is draining. Extroverted mothers with small children need adult interaction, time with their husbands, and social activities. Interaction with adults, conversations with adults, socializing, and sharing charge their batteries.

We seldom marry somebody just like us. In my forty years as a marriage counselor, I've rarely seen a couple where both had the exact same score on the introvert-extrovert scale. This means that even if both parties in the relationship are extroverts, one may still feel the need for more social interaction than their partner. I'm right smack in the middle of being both an extrovert and an introvert. Bonnie is very much a social-interactive person. She doesn't like public speaking or large crowds, but it feeds her soul to be interacting with people. So we take two cars to church because she likes to stay until she has talked to as many people as she can. I like to shake hands, say hello or good-bye, and then I'm out of there. Too much social interaction drains me. The longer Bonnie socially interacts, the stronger and more energized she becomes, while I'm withering like a dwindling plant in the background.

The best way to figure out each other's needs is to talk about them. We could ask, "Do you need a certain amount of alone time?" We often tend to interpret a person going into himself or herself as going away from us when the he or she may just need some alone time. It's important to realize there's a difference between someone going *into themselves* and that person *going away* from us.

We can look at it this way. Perhaps a social man's job doesn't fill any of his social needs. He might want to come home and then go do something, but the woman might be a little more introverted, having worked hard herself, and just wants to stay home. Or, typically, it's reversed. We have a man who's just come home; he feels like the bad guys are pursuing him, and he's riding home to the fort where he can rest and be safe from them. But when he gets home, his wife says that the bad guys are *in* the fort. She's been with them all day, and she's looking for some social interaction because talking to the little bad guys doesn't count. Can you see a conflict of needs here?

This is where content communicating works well. We need straight talk, questions like, "What are your needs here?" In his book *Thank God— It's Monday!* (New York: Bantam, 1985), Dr. Pierre Hornell, a psychiatrist from UCLA, talks about urban professionals who are highly successful at work but aren't doing well in their personal relationships. They're grateful when Monday comes so they can be successful because when they go home on the weekends, their relationships are a disaster. Much of the reason for their professional success is that their roles in the workplace are clearly defined. The home front, however, is a different story. Hornell says that in order for personal relationships to work, we need to be able to come home and not get hit with a list of problems when we walk in the door. We need to have a transition time.

So, extrovert or introvert, a person's going to need some transition time. If a man is an introvert, alone time is where he can have an emotional release and not feel that he's resented for having that alone time.

Defining Expectations

One woman complained that her husband spent too much time watching television and too much time on the computer. I asked her what she meant by that. She explained that he spent five hours a night in front of the computer or the television. And I said I didn't see what was wrong. She said, "Well, don't you think that's too much?" I told her I didn't. Now, I need to clarify one thing. I understand that there was a riot in Alpine, Utah, following my seminar—that women were marching in the streets because Dr. Lund said men could watch five hours of television. I want to retract that. I meant six hours of television. Then she said, "Well, he never talks to me." So the real issue was spending quality time together. She assumed that if he spent less time in front of the television and less time at the computer, he'd talk to her more. This is a great example of a woman who runs the risk of parenting her husband in order to have her need of more "talk time" met. There is a difference between defining our needs for someone, and defining *them*. Defining them is a parent's job. Telling them what they should, need, or ought to do—trying to control all aspects of their life—is a parent's job. Now, this particular woman thought that her husband would talk to her more if he watched less television. In her brain, the two things were related.

I quickly explained that he'd simply find something else if he didn't watch TV, model planes maybe. I then asked her, "Why would he want to talk to you?" And she replied, "Well, I don't feel like we have a relationship. And if we are going to have a relationship, then we need to talk." I asked her, "How much talking time a night would be enough?" This is where content communication is so wonderful.

The issue wasn't that her husband watched five hours of television. The issue was his wife's unwillingness or inability to define her needs for him. What did she want from him? She figured if she dropped enough hints, if she complained about how much television he was watching, he'd figure it out. But we already know how counterproductive nagging and hint dropping can be.

This woman was trying to fill a void, and she thought that by defining her husband, she would be able to have more of her needs met. The truth was, she needed to identify her expectations clearly. If she defined what she needed from him, she would have a better opportunity for success than in trying to restrict his behaviors. She needed to try something like this: "Honey, I really feel the need to be able to talk with you every night for at least a few minutes. Could we have fifteen minutes a night? I promise that fifteen minutes is not a springboard into two hours. It's fifteen minutes." Now that's called credibility. Fifteen minutes means fifteen minutes.

Remember, men tend to be defensive. If a woman approaches a man with, "Can we talk? You can tell me about your day; I'll tell you about mine." This man is going to be a little leery and defensive about an open-ended conversation. He's thinking, *You're just going to find an opening to tell me why I am not fit as a husband, father, or human being because I watch too much television and spend too much time on the computer.*

This particular story had a number of positive outcomes. They both agreed to be content communicators. She was delighted when he agreed to spend fifteen minutes a night just talking. He was delighted that she stopped nagging and complaining and simply identified her needs in very specific terms with each need having an exit.

Not only do men tend to be defensive but, also, as pointed out earlier, men look for exits. In one study I participated in at the University of Washington, we took a group of one hundred men and women, fifty of each, into the Hec Edmunson Pavilion and asked for their opinions on a pseudo-issue. We really wanted to test their subconscious awareness of their physical surroundings. A week later, around ninety-seven of them returned to a different location and were asked about the room they were in a week earlier. One of the questions we asked them was, "Which direction was north from where you were seated in the building, and where were the exits in that room?" Less than 20 percent of the women knew where any of the exits were. Over 80 percent of the men nailed every exit in the building and knew where north was. What is there about men that they are aware of exits? Why are men accused of having a hard time of committing? It's because men are reluctant to commit until they can see an exit or clearly understand the boundaries. The more open-ended something is, the more difficult it is for a man to commit. Men are reluctant to enter a building or a conversation that has no exit or clearly defined boundary.

So when a woman asks, "Can we talk?" there are no exits. The man is thinking, *This is a black hole into which I am going to fall and never recover.* Men need exits. Women can try something like this: "Honey, can we talk for fifteen minutes—and I mean fifteen minutes? I don't mean twenty, and I don't mean thirty; it would mean a lot to me if we could just talk for fifteen minutes. It's not painful." The chances of a man refusing to talk are going to be greater the more open-ended a woman is.

Here's how Bonnie and I, as content communicators, would approach a request for help with a project: Bonnie says, "Could you help me for forty-five minutes on Saturday cleaning out the garage?"

My reply: "Honey, I really wanted to watch that ball game."

She says, "We could start at 8:00, and be done by 8:45. That's all I ask of you on Saturday. If it's not done in forty-five minutes, I'll get someone else to help, or you can do it at another time."

"Okay, let's make it an hour and a half, as long as I can be in front of the TV by 10:00 AM."

I'm going to be much more responsive if I have a clear idea of the expectation. It has an entrance; it has an exit. If forty-five minutes is a ploy to get me involved on a project that is going to last five hours, she will have a hard time getting me to agree to any future commitment. As a content communicator, forty-five minutes is forty-five minutes, unless otherwise agreed upon.

Bonnie and I made an agreement, because we have eight children, that I would give her one hour of labor per child still living at home, and I would perform the labor with a good attitude on the weekdays or on a Saturday. However, after I met that particular commitment, I was free to pursue my own activities with the kids or work on a project, and she would support me with a good attitude.

As we'll discuss in the next chapter, it's important to be able to define "enough." Because if we are a bottomless pit, and our spouse gives everything he or she can, and we still feel it's not enough, why should that spouse feel motivated to give anything? We're still going to be frustrated and resentful no matter what our spouse gives.

The challenge is to be a content communicator with credibility—we mean what we say, and we say it straight. When I would show up and ask Bonnie what she'd like me to do for eight hours (one hour for each of our eight children), she usually handed me a 3x5 card with enough work projects to keep an army of men working for a month. I would ask, "Are there any projects in particular you want me to work on, or do you want me to start at the top and go for as long as I can?"

She would say, "Yes, that's what I would like you to do."

To which I responded, "But after that, if I want to waste my time, you know, just sit and watch four football games in a row or play computer games with the children, I don't want you walking by, saying, 'There's so much to do and so few hands to do it. You could be folding socks, you know, while you are just sitting there wasting your time in unproductive ways."

When we talk about having an expectation, we have to ask ourselves who owns that expectation. Does the husband have the expectation that a small couch needs to be moved? If it's the wife who wants the couch moved, she needs to own that expectation. It's important not to transfer the responsibility for an expectation we have and resent that others don't have that same expectation. We can make a request, and then if it doesn't happen, we can talk about an alternative. We can negotiate for its fulfillment.

What if the wife negotiates and the husband still doesn't follow through? There needs to be some give-and-take. The following true story of a plumber and his wife illustrates this point. This plumber and his wife had a family of nine. They had three toilets in their home, and one of these toilets was broken, and so the plumber had shut it off. He'd been fixing other people's toilets all day, and when he came home, his frustrated wife said, "You're a plumber; fix the toilet, for heaven's sake. You know we have a big family here, and you're not here all day. We're crammed into just two bathrooms. The kids have to use our bathroom, and you don't like it when they make a mess in there. You need to get this fixed." It became World War III between them.

The husband said, "I just want to relax. I don't want to have to come home and jump right in and start doing the things I've been doing all day."

Then she reminded him of their negotiations. They had agreed that she would ask him one time to fix something and then remind him one time. If he didn't respond, she would hire it out. "Listen, honey, I've asked you one time, and I've reminded you one time. Are you okay with that?"

He said, "I am okay with that, because I would rather not be nagged for a year about it. It's worth it to me to have you hire someone else."

Now, that was how they negotiated. She can ask once, and she can remind once, and if it's not taken care by that time, the wife can go ahead and have someone else do it. Maybe the husband would rather work an extra half hour and pay that person to do it anyway.

Here's an example of how Bonnie and I use negotiation. Early in our marriage, every time Bonnie would see me, she would ask me to take care of a dozen details, little things that needed to be done. I finally said, "Honey, you are driving me crazy with these endless requests of things you want me to do. Would you just write them down and put them on the refrigerator?" Well, pretty soon, she had four sheets of paper on the fridge, Scotch-taped together. When you closed the fridge door, it was like waving a flag. On a Saturday, when Bonnie was gone, I hired this fix-it guy, because on the side of his van it said, "I fix anything." And it had a big number. So I called the number and said, "Do you do odd jobs like this?" I read a few of the things on the list.

He laughed and said, "Yeah, that's what I do. I'm a fix-it guy."

So I had him come on a Saturday, a half hour after Bonnie had left for a Young Women activity.

Now, I enjoy writing. So I went into my office, and I wrote while the fix-it man took care of the four-page list on the refrigerator door. Let me tell you what this list was like: "Replace the screw in the screen door. It has come out the top, and we need a larger screw in the top hinge of the screen door." "The carpet is coming out where you come in the door, and that little lippy thing needs to be tucked under or whatever you do to get that fixed, but that needs to be taken care of. That's a potential hazard." Ad nauseam. Multiply that by twenty. Bonnie's dad was a Mr. Fix-It guy. So according to Bonnie, that's what men do. They take out the garbage, they take care of the yard work, keep the cars in running order, and do this other fix-it stuff. That's what men do. Bonnie was very good with details, and so all four sheets were very detailed.

Every once in a while I'd hear the fix-it man go in the kitchen to read the next item on the list and laugh. Of course, he was thinking, *Any moron could do this, and you're paying me to do it.* But I didn't mind. I enjoyed it. I was in hog-heaven doing my writing. I was doing what I enjoyed doing. I had a great Saturday. The fix-it man left completely exhausted before Bonnie returned, but he did it all—everything on the list. All four sheets—gone. Best money I ever spent. My wife came home, and the first thing she did was put her hand on the screen door to open it, and she saw that the screw was fixed. She walked around; the carpet was fixed. She was ecstatic. The leaky faucet wasn't dripping; the screen on the front window was repaired. Her every expectation had been met! All four pages! She came into the room where I was writing and said, "Oh, honey, you must be so tired after all those projects. I'm so grateful. Thank you! Thank you! Thank you!"

Later, I heard her on the phone bragging to her friends about everything I had accomplished. I didn't have the heart to confess that I'd hired somebody to do it. So I accepted full credit and basked in her love and adoration for two weeks.

It was about the time she was bragging to the fiftieth person about all the fix-it stuff I'd done that my conscience finally got the better of me. I said, "Honey, I didn't do all that. I actually hired a fix-it man." You'd have thought I had committed adultery. It was her expectation that *I* do the jobs. After all, in her value system, it was a part of my job description. But it didn't take long for Bonnie to see the wisdom of my actions. She was happy that the list had been taken care of; I was happy that I'd been able to spend my time writing. Now Bonnie's priorities are, "I don't care who does the work, as long as the work gets done. Bring on the fix-it man."

CHAPTER FIVE

The Challenge—Managing the Negative in Our Relationships

There probably is no other place where it's stated more profoundly than in the gospel of Jesus Christ that *how* we approach something is as important as *what* we are doing. Jesus identified Himself as *the way,* not just "the *what*" we were to do (see John 14:6). And we will never, ever carry out the Lord's program in the devil's way. We will never achieve a righteous cause with an unrighteous method.

Unfortunately, many of us, as a part of our culture and family traditions, have picked up a hypercritical attitude. Some families are super sarcastic. We call it being witty, but it's really quite negative in terms of the criticism we allow to sneak into our everyday conversations.

I often challenge my students to see if they can go for twenty-four hours without criticizing any person for any reason. This includes other drivers, the government, anybody. This even includes self-criticism. Ironically, many of my students make their first mistake before they've even left the building. The rule is, if they let any criticism slip, they have to begin the twenty-four hour period over until they complete one consecutive twenty-four-hour period without criticism.

I had a great experience in Anaheim, California, with this twenty-four-hour challenge. A man and a woman came up to me after the seminar, and the woman said, "Dr. Lund, if you think it but you don't say it, does it count?" I said, "If you dwell upon that negative thought for more than thirty seconds, yes, you have to start your twenty-four hours over again. But if the thought comes into your mind, and you wrestle with it, and you kick it out, no, you don't have to start over again." This woman looked at her husband and said, "I'll try, but he'll never make it." All six-plus feet of him looked down at her five-foot stature, and then he shook his finger at her. And I said to him, "That's nonverbal criticizing." Then I turned to her and said, "And you just criticized him." As she walked away she said, "This is going to be a lot harder than I thought." There are exceptions, of course. If we encounter a life-or-death situation, or if we're prompted by the Holy Spirit, "reproving betimes with sharpness," we can offer some criticism (see D&C 121:43). But most of the time, we're moved upon by frustration, by our unmet expectations, and not by the Spirit.

It's not easy. Bonnie and I tried it years ago in our own marriage. Bonnie was able to do it in one week. In one week she found twenty-four consecutive hours where she didn't criticize anyone for any reason. It took me three weeks. And you know why? It happened every time I got behind the wheel. I am situationally critical, and that situation brings out the beast in me. I was saying, "Dumb driver," "Look at that idiot," and "On what planet did he learn to drive?" Bonnie would just look at me, and I'd say, "Oh. I've got to start over again." Sometimes I would have twenty-two hours logged and during a one-mile drive to the store I would be critical of another driver, and so it was back to minute number one.

Now, I didn't expect my students to live the rest of their lives that way. But I wanted them to see if they could go for twenty-four hours without criticizing anyone. And the reason was so that they could experience two things: One was so they could see how much they'd allowed a critical disposition to take over their communication patterns. And two, so they'd realize how difficult it was to abstain from criticism. During the April 2007 general conference, Elder Jeffrey R. Holland of the Quorum of the Twelve said that one of the commandments Latter-day Saints break most often is that we are not of "good cheer," as the Lord instructed in John 16:33. It's hard to have a heart filled with criticism and good cheer at the same time.

Family Prayer Scenario

We often learn the most from our mistakes. Family prayer was just such an opportunity for me in learning how *not* to handle things. I never seemed to find the right time for family prayer. I'm supposed to be the spiritual leader and patriarchal father in the home, so I tried to get the children together for family prayer. And my wife said, "Well, honey, it's probably not a good time right now. In about five minutes one of the kids will be home, and another child is just finishing his homework assignment, and . . ." I don't know how many times I tried to gather the family, to no avail. So at a certain point, I thought, *Never mind, I'm not going to try. Every time I try I get put down.* Am I supposed to tune into karma and find out when the exact right time for family prayer is? That's not realistic. How do we solve that?

My first inclination was to say, "Fine. Why don't you just wear the pants in the family?" Though I saw my role as patriarch hanging in the balance, I let go of my pride a little and said, "Honey, I don't always know when the best time is, but I would appreciate your support on this. So why don't you suggest when a good time would be, and then I'll call everyone to family prayer." Now maybe that time varied, and Bonnie would come and say, "This might be a good time for family prayer." It worked. My initial problem with her suggesting anything was the sense that if she had to remind me, I must be a failure. The problem was that I was interpreting her "suggestion" as a sign of my inadequacy. And it's not about being inadequate; it's about working together and letting her be a helpmate. It's about being supportive. So Bonnie would come and say, "This is a good time." And I would then say, "Kids, this is a great time for family prayer; let's get together." And Bonnie and I worked as one.

And that wasn't the only struggle I had with family prayer. I used to think, *We are going to family prayer, and we are going to get everybody there, and, by darn, we are going to have a good spirit whether we want to or not.* This was all about free agency and how to enforce it.

It happened when I was serving as bishop in Moscow, Idaho. I remember calling the family to prayer after Bonnie's suggestion. Now, there were several children doing different things, and we were calling them together. The ones who were quickly obedient were now waiting for those who were dragging their feet. And pretty soon we were waiting and waiting for everybody to come to family prayer. Five-year-old David was down the hall refusing to come, and he was holding us all hostage to family prayer. This five year old was delighting in his power. And I was beginning to froth at the mouth, and my eyes turned glassy, and, of course, we were going to have a spiritual experience.

Finally, out of frustration, I marched down the hall and picked him up. It was February in Moscow, Idaho, and really cold. I opened the door, put him on the porch, and said, "Go find a family that wants you. We don't want you anymore if you are not going to come to family prayer." And I slammed the door. I turned around and saw Bonnie and the other kids staring at me with their hands on their hips. I wasn't going to leave him there. I opened the door, and he said, "I'll come in to family prayer."

"Good," I huffed. "I hope we've all learned something from this. We will now pray and have a good spirit."

I've apologized about forty thousand times to this little boy who is now thirty-six years old and has a five year old of his own. David finally said, "Dad, stop apologizing. I only remember it because you keep telling me the story, but I forgave you a long time ago. I never really felt bad about it. It's okay, let it go." I think the reason I had a hard time letting it go was that I pictured myself showing up in heaven and Heavenly Father saying, "Oh, it's you. Go find a family who loves you. We don't want you anymore."

Sometimes we try to carry out the Lord's program in the devil's way. But it never works. After that, I announced to the family that, periodically, all those who came to family prayer within two minutes of being called would receive as a treat an ice-cream cone. It wouldn't be every night and it might be two days in a row and go for ten days without ice cream. It was arbitrary and they would never know. A couple of times those who came to family prayer on time would sneak out of the house with me and we would push the car down the road so no one could hear it being started as we left to go enjoy an ice-cream cone. It was at those times that the child who missed would say, "Well if I knew you were going to have ice cream I would have come." A popular phrase at that time was "bummer deal." But maybe the greatest lesson I learned about family prayer was that it was better to have Bonnie and myself and three or four of the children and to have a good spiritual experience than it was to become a frustrated parent and try to have family prayer without the Spirit.

Some people have questioned the ice-cream-for-family-prayer program. "Dr. Lund, aren't you bribing them?" No, because a bribe is illegal and immoral. A reward is not. In a spirit of gentleness and persuasion, they were motivated to come for family prayer. Remember, the Lord has promised us great rewards for our obedience and faithful service. "How oft have I called upon you by the mouth of my servants, and . . . by the voice of glory and honor and the riches of eternal life" (D&C 43:25).

Great Initiator—Great Responder

What happens if my needs or wishes are constantly ignored even when I have clearly communicated and done so in a kind manner?

Although we have clearly communicated as a content communicator, there is the expectation that people are to remember everything we have communicated at the time it is important to us. Remember our earlier discussion about how all frustration comes from unmet expectations? *Ownership of our expectations does not end once we have communicated them clearly and with kindness.* There is a key element that makes content communication successful. We must assume that the significant others in our life—all of them—have Alzheimer's. They do not remember everything that is important to us. This principle involves owning your expectations in the present. The following story illustrates this point.

I had the expectation that Bonnie would greet me with a hug and a kiss when I came home. She might remember on one out of five days and, of course, I felt miserable and rejected the other four days. Sometimes weeks would go by, and we would finally wind up in tears at 3:00 AM, each wondering if we had married the wrong person and each of us feeling inadequate and unappreciated. All of this was due to my expectation of being greeted with a hug and a kiss when I got home. I felt I had clearly and kindly expressed my desire, and yet she did not remember. Why? If our relationship was so important, why could she not remember to give me just fifteen seconds of her time five days a week? Before I answer that question, I would like you to understand where my expectation came from.

I grew up during World War II. My four aunts and two grandmothers raised a group of five boys throughout the war. I was eleven months old when Pearl Harbor was bombed. And my dad and all my uncles were called up to action, except one uncle who didn't qualify. He stayed and worked in a munitions factory. All during those war years—about five-and-a-half years—I remember that every day before my uncle came home, about fifteen minutes before he arrived, my aunt put her hair up, rolling it in a bun. And she put on bright-red lipstick. She wore pants during the day, but she changed into what was called a housedress, and then she hovered by the front door until he came home. When she saw him walking up the sidewalk, she stepped out on the front porch, threw her arms around him, and gave him a big kiss. And he picked her up and twirled her around. And I was a little boy watching this during those formative years between being a toddler and a kindergartener. This impression was seared into my childhood mind. I began to think, *When I get married, that's what my wife is going to do. She's going to hover at the front door, waiting for her man to come home.*

Then the reality of marriage hit me. Bonnie was not about to hover. We had eight children. She was too busy to hover at the door waiting for me to come home. Bonnie didn't have time to hover anywhere. I didn't always get home at the same time everyday like my uncle did, and she couldn't sit around waiting for me, not with eight children running around. The "hovering at the front door" expectation would have to be buried, along with a dozen other nice but unrealistic expectations. However, I would forget those small details, and I came to the insane conclusion that if Bonnie really cared she wouldn't let anything stop her from greeting me with a hug and a kiss. If she truly loved me, she'd remember how important it was to me and always do it. I concluded that she never really did love me and that I probably married the wrong person.

Insanity? That was where my thinking was taking me. There is no question that Bonnie loved me; she always has. But we often feel that if we have to ask someone we love for something we want and it doesn't happen, we are not loved. That is dysfunctional. It's important to realize how unrealistic those kinds of expectations are. And we must learn to let them go. They are artificial and false tests of love.

We must come to *own our realistic expectations* in the present. So when I came home, I would call out in a loud voice, "I'm home! I'm here for a hug and a kiss." I no longer expected Bonnie to come to me; I went to her, and she was happy to greet me with the kind of affection I needed. And after nearly forty-five years of marriage, Bonnie still doesn't remember, but I'm not frustrated because I don't expect her to remember. What was and is important to me is for Bonnie to be a great responder—to greet me with a hug and a kiss after I own my expectation. My requiring Bonnie to remember was setting her up for failure, and it was certainly setting me up for frustration.

What if we could take memory out as an expectation? I loved Bonnie; Bonnie loved me, but she didn't always remember. I was making *memory* the issue and not *loving and being loved.* There was one big hurdle to overcome before I could let go. I felt she was supposed to "initiate" the loving behavior. But what if I removed "initiating" from the expectations as well? Both *memory* and the expectation that she would *initiate* the hug and the kiss were still setting both of us up for disaster. Wait! What if Bonnie is a great responder and I'm a great initiator? After all, it is my expectation and I need to own it. So I let go of my expectations for *memory* as a sign of love and *initiation* as a token of love. I replaced them both by owning my expectations in the moment of my need. Bonnie agreed to be a great responder and I agreed to be a great initiator. This allowed love and affection to get through the barriers of unrealistic expectations. Yes, I had to let go of symbols that once seemed important, but, in reality, it was the substance of love I really wanted. It was the acceptance I felt in her embrace, it was the affection I felt in her kiss that was infinitely more important than her remembering or initiating. Now when I come home, I continue to say, "Honey, I'm home. I'm here for a hug and kiss." This is called initiating.

We must own our expectations in the present. "It would mean a lot to me if . . ." "I would appreciate it if . . ." It's naïve to think that our spouse will always remember everything that's important to us. It's safer to stay away from the mentality that requires another person to process all our values exactly as we think they ought to. Again, we must be willing to own our expectations in the present. So, we are going to communicate our expectations clearly with kindness and initiate what it is we need to take place on a daily or hourly basis, if necessary. All of this is a part of being a content communicator.

It's important to give ourselves and those we love credit for initiating or responding. And even though Bonnie may never initiate, or even think about it—she receives full credit for being a great responder. It doesn't matter which one we are. If I initiate fifty things and Bonnie initiates one, that's still great initiating and responding. Is it not true that a loving response is as important as a loving invitation? And maybe the actual behavior of a loving response is more significant than the verbal request which initiates it.

CHAPTER SIX

Acceptance, Affection, and Appreciation

In order to overcome these barriers to communication and to become great initiators and great responders, it's important we understand the different ways people give and receive messages of love and acceptance. Now, it's commonly known that different people have different learning styles. Some learn by auditory means. This means their mouths and ears are the dominant sources of their learning abilities. We used to think that all people learned 80 percent visually and 20 percent auditory, but we know now that's not true. Some are visual learners, and some are kinetic, or tactile.

Let's say I want to teach three children what a five is. Now, for a visual child, I might show him or her a five and say, "This is a five." I could verbally describe it to an auditory learner, but for the tactile child, I might make a five out of wood and actually take the child's fingers and have him *feel* what a five is. The tactile child, feeling a five, will engrave it in his memory.

We also know that people have different learning styles when it comes to love. There are different ways people have learned to interpret love. For our purposes, we are going to take the word *love* and translate it into a few other words—*acceptance, affection,* and *appreciation.* And we'll talk about how people send and receive messages of love—messages of acceptance, affection, and appreciation. These messages of love are also known as love languages. I wrote my first book in 1980, entitled *Avoiding Emotional Divorce,* dealing with love language. Legal divorce is almost always preceded by people who have grown out of love and who have emotionally divorced. By learning each other's love language, we can avoid becoming emotionally divorced.

In a class on communication and relationships for married students I taught at the University of Utah, I had husbands and wives sit knee-to-knee, blindfolded. Then I told them I wanted them to communicate acceptance to one another. Most reached out to pat each other on the shoulder. Then I'd tell them I wanted them to communicate affection. More than half the time, those who were touch-oriented kissed the other person. Much of the time, the recipient of the kiss would say, "You didn't say we could use our lips." The thought had never even entered the touch-oriented person's mind. That's the point. We have different ways of processing things depending on what we have learned.

Ninety-five percent of people want to send and receive messages of acceptance, affection, and appreciation in the same language. I did meet a couple where the man wanted to send messages in the language of touch and receive them in a visual manner—he showed people he loved them with one kind of behavior, but he wanted to be shown in quite a different behavior how he was appreciated. About 5 percent of the population falls into that category. That is, they send in one love language and receive in another. But generally, we tend to show people love the same way we want them to show us love.

I had another couple that came to me who had been married fifty-one years (not the same couple with the communication challenges in an earlier chapter). And I remember how frustrated they were. I asked them if they understood each other's love language. I explained that we tend to interpret other people's behaviors through the filter of our own eyes, our own feelings, and our own value systems. I explained that each person's love language is quite distinct, and that the best way to figure out our mate's love language is to notice how they treat those they love. It's like using the golden rule as a measuring stick.

Love Language Quiz

During my classes, I would have my students take a twenty-seven-question quiz called the "Love Language Quiz." I would instruct class members to choose just one of three options, A, B, or C, in each set of questions and to choose only one answer, even if more than one answer applied to them.

In order to determine which love language you speak, I've included the quiz in this chapter. Let's help people figure us out. Remember, in taking the quiz, it's important to answer the questions based on your first impression. (You can download more copies from my web site: www.drlund.com. Look under "quizzes.")

1. Are you a) a deeply feeling person, b) a talking-sharing person, or c) a doing-showing person?
2. The thing I remember receiving most in my childhood was a) affection, b) verbal praise, or c) rewards.
3. The family I grew up in demonstrated love by a) touching, b) telling each other, or c) it was just understood.

4. As a child I remember being a) spanked, b) yelled at, or c) grounded. (If none of these things happened, which one would you have feared the most?)
5. People need to be more considerate of a) other people's feelings, b) how they speak to each other, or c) other people's time and schedules.
6. In communicating affection to my mate, I prefer to a) give tender kisses, b) express tender words, or c) give a gift of tender meaning.
7. I would most enjoy receiving from my companion a) a hug and a kiss, b) an opportunity to talk about the day's events, or c) a phone call during the day. (And I know that you want them all, but choose one. It'll work out.)
8. For a small gift, I would most enjoy receiving a) a coupon that said, "Good for one backrub or foot massage," b) a personal handwritten letter expressing appreciation, or c) a chance to work with my spouse on a favorite project.
9. I am most frustrated by a) insensitive people, b) critical people, or c) unfair people.
10. I need to spend more time with my mate talking about a) positive things, b) significant events, or c) alternatives and solutions.
11. I would prefer a) walking hand in hand, b) a positive, heart-to-heart talk, or c) a clean house or well-kept yard.
12. It is more important to have my mate a) sit next to me, b) talk about my hopes and dreams, or c) remember to run an errand for me.
13. I would rather be a) embraced and treated affectionately, b) told that I am loved, or c) shown that I am loved.
14. What I admire in a friend is a) unconditional acceptance, b) availability and understanding, or c) loyalty and dependability.
15. I would prefer to have my mate a) reach out and touch me, b) say I love you, or c) surprise me with a good deed.
16. My idea of a great weekend is a) spending time just being together, b) visiting with friends and family, or c) getting lots of projects accomplished.
17. I would prefer receiving appreciation by a) a hug, b) a kind word, or c) receiving something I need.
18. With which of these statements would you most agree? a) I would rather hold hands in public or walk arm-in-arm and mean it than live in a fancy house. b) I would rather be told I was loved than be married to a workaholic who is always giving me everything but himself or herself. c) You shouldn't have to tell people you love them; they should know it by the way they're treated.

19. The thing that upsets me most about children is their a) not being affectionate, b) talking back, or c) not being obedient.

20. The thing that upsets me most about my loved one is their a) lack of intimacy, b) failure to communicate, or c) lack of responsibility.

21. I would rather have my mate a) be physically expressive in touching, b) recognize my efforts with words of appreciation, or c) demonstrate appreciation by doing something I can see.

22. When I get upset as a parent, I am more inclined to a) spank, b) scold, or c) withdraw privileges. (We are talking about being reasonable in all of this, not abusive behavior.)

23. As a parent of a young child, I would prefer a) holding or wrestling with them, b) reading a story to them, or c) taking them to the park. (It's not about what you think *they* would like, it's what *you* would prefer to do.)

24. I feel good a) just being held (We're not talking about an intimate relationship), b) being able to fully express myself, or c) getting things done.

25. Which best describes you? a) physically expressive, b) verbally expressive, or c) accomplishment oriented.

26. As a sign of caring for me, I would like to receive from my loved ones a) lots of affection, b) sincere praise, or c) hands-on help.

27. I would prefer to have my mate a) spend more one-on-one time with me, b) pay me a compliment, or c) show greater participation in doing daily tasks.

Love Language Quiz Results

In order to score the quiz and determine your value system, count up the number of A's, B's, and C's. Whichever letter you have the most of, that's your dominant love language, or what you most value. If you scored mostly A's, you're a touch person. If you chose mostly B's, you're a verbal person, and if you had mostly C's, you're a visual person. It helps us to understand this love-language concept if we think of these love languages as foreign languages. We'll say the touch language is Spanish. We'll say the verbal is Japanese, and the visual, German. By the way, 50 percent of the population has A as their highest number. Thirty-five percent of the population has B, and 15 percent has C as their highest number. And if we break it down further, we find that 50 percent of all touch people are male, 50 percent female.

If we look at the male/female ratio in the verbal category, we'll see a two-to-one difference—about 65 women to 35 men. I happen to be a verbal man, meaning that Bonnie would just as soon not argue with me because I could win the argument even if I were wrong. And lastly, half of all visuals are men, half women. Bonnie is a visual. She scored 3-3-21. Three A's, three B's and twenty-one C's. This woman speaks German. And what is not surprising is that I scored 12-12-3.

So, a 3-3-21 marries a 12-12-3. Bonnie is inclined to say, "A little less huggy-wuggy, a little less talkie-walkie, and a lot more dooey-wooey." I once had a student who had eleven touch, five verbal, and eleven visual. He showed his family love by what he *did* for them, but he wanted to be appreciated by touch and affection.

In order to determine your dominant love language, take a look at your highest number. If that number is a ten, twelve, or fourteen, that's your language. It's never happened that someone was a 27-0-0. Sometimes the challenge is that the person close to you may have three numbers that almost match. We call these universal donors. If there's anyone who needs to clearly communicate their expectations, it's a 9-9-9 or a combination close to that. There may be some who are within one or two of being the same. These folks need balance. That is why the 9-9-9 is very significant. We may think of these as cups that need to be filled—three nine-ounce cups. So Bonnie has twenty-one ounces to fill in one cup and only three ounces in the other two. I have to give twenty-one ounces to her visual cup. But my inclination as a verbal-touch guy is to want to put all of my love and affection into the first two cups—touch and verbal. Won't Bonnie be happy with a hug and kiss and talking about wonderful things?

What's funny is that Bonnie wants to talk about scheduling what we need to do and what needs to get done, but I want to talk about fluff. I don't want to talk about serious stuff all the time. This has caused a few problems. I'm thinking, *Let's talk about that cabin I want in Park City.*

I've wanted a cabin in Park City all our married life. We don't have one yet. But I like to talk about wanting a cabin in Park City. Bonnie wants to talk about getting things done. *Productivity* and *accomplishment* are her key words. For her, most weekends are big projects—get the wallpapering done, paint the house. What energizes her absolutely saps my energy. And what amazes me about Bonnie is that the more we get done, the more she is energized—let's clean the garage; let's get out there and really get it organized. So all day, for maybe eight or ten hours, we clean the garage. But there's still daylight when we're done. And Bonnie says, "Oh, honey, you don't want to stop now. Let's go to the barn." One of the problems with visuals is that they see what *hasn't* been done—they see the little dirt spot on the floor and fail to notice that you cleaned the windows. So visuals have to be very careful about commenting on what hasn't been done and make a special point to acknowledge what has been accomplished.

Love Language and Music

I once asked one of my students at the university to help me do a study to see if there was any correlation between love languages and the songs people preferred. We asked touch, verbal, and visual people what their favorite songs were. We looked at country-western music, pop music, and LDS hymns. And the results were absolutely amazing. More than half of those we surveyed selected songs consistent with their value systems. And we found that about one-third of the hymns in the LDS hymnbook are touchy-feely hymns, one-third are verbal ("Nay, Speak No Ill"; "Let Us Oft Speak Kind Words"), and one-third are visual ("Have I Done Any Good?").

Let's take hymn number 223, "Have I Done Any Good?" to illustrate how the value system is reflected in hymn choice. Think about a visual's value system and the emphasis on doing.

Have I *done* any good in the world today?
Have I *helped* anyone in need?
Have I *cheered up* the sad and *made* someone feel glad?
If not, I have failed indeed.
Has anyone's burden *been lighter* today
Because I was *willing to share*?
Have the sick and the weary been *helped* on their way?
When they needed my help *was I there*?
Then *wake up* and *do* something more
Than dream of your [cabin in Park City].
Doing good is a pleasure, a joy beyond measure,
A blessing of *duty* and love.

Duty is such a big word for visuals. Listen to the second verse:

There are chances for *work* all around just now,
Opportunities right in our way.
Do not let them pass by, saying, "Sometime I'll try,"
But *go* and *do* something today.
'Tis noble of man to *work* and to *give*;
Love's *labor* has merit alone.
Only he who *does* something *helps* others to live.
To God each good *work* will be known.

Originally, the second to the last line read, "Only he who does some-thing is worthy to live. The world has no need for the drone." I'm a drone.

Isn't that amazing? In the original song you're not even worthy to *live* if you don't *do* something! Now, why is this song any more important than "Let Us Oft Speak Kind Words to Each Other"? It's not, unless you are a visual. Even the songs we sing tend to reflect our love language. Would you like to know which of all the hymns was Bonnie's favorite as she was growing up and which is still one of her favorite hymns today? "Have I Done Any Good in the World Today?"

CHAPTER SEVEN

Defining Enough

One of the keys to success in learning each other's love language is in defining enough. With Bonnie being a 21 visual, when will she think I have done enough? Never! But in all fairness to Bonnie, we have never reached *enough* for my touch personality. We touch everyday, and I am not talking about sexual things. I mean holding hands, hugging, sitting by each other, her touching me on the arm as she passes by, etc. I'm talking about the confirmation of our love for each other and the value that comes with such confirmation.

Bonnie knows she will never have talked enough for me, either. The thing that's ironic, though, is that Bonnie knows when I want to talk, I want to talk about the cabin in Park City. At the first of our marriage she was afraid I was going to run out and buy this cabin, which we couldn't afford. What she didn't realize then was that I just wanted to dream. I've been dreaming for forty-five years now, and that's okay. And here's the message in this: Don't be a dream killer. Let those who dream, dream. And let reality kill the dream. There is great wisdom in that. It's important to be able to dream our dreams. The world is filled with dream killers, and yet, some dreams do come true. We need not be irresponsible and rush out and spend money we don't have on our dreams. However, we can let reality kill the dream because most of the time reality does kill it. If you are the one who kills the dream, you may always carry the title of "dream killer," regardless of your good intent or pure motives.

If Bonnie says, "I'm going to save you from yourself in having that dream. I'm going to remind you of our reality. We can't afford a cabin in Park City; we couldn't afford to even buy the lot. I'm going to be a huge, soggy, wet blanket of reality falling out of the sky onto your little fire of hope," she becomes a dream killer. And then I start to resent *her* as the symbol of reality.

It's important not to be seen on the negative side of the dream. So Bonnie has learned to let me talk.

Returning to love languages, the key lies in defining *enough*—what is enough touching, enough talking, enough doing. It's never enough, but we must own the expectation of how much is enough for now. Maybe in a week or month or a year things will change, but for now this is enough touching, enough talking, and enough doing. We must clearly identify in specific terms and measurable behaviors what enough is. The consequences for not doing so are frustration and unmet expectations. It is unattractive to be a person who is always frustrated. And it certainly is hard to feel love or acceptance from a person who is always frustrated.

Remember, I promised Bonnie a certain number of hours of labor. However, after I'd given my time, that was to be enough. Then, if I wanted to waste my time or squander it in what, according to Bonnie, were unproductive pursuits, she would support me with a good attitude. If I wanted to simply sit eating popcorn and watching football, I could. What I didn't want from Bonnie was the nonacceptance message: "You could be folding stockings, you know; you're just sitting there wasting time. You could be doing something productive instead of just wasting all that time. There is so much to do and so few hands to do it."

We are talking about meeting realistic expectations. If I *do* something for Bonnie, it's a big *I love you* for her. For example, in addition to my normal chores, I make a special effort to clean the kitchen. With everything that needs to be done, Bonnie, as a visual, is inclined to think, *Well, cleaning the kitchen—that was good. There is more to do, but that was good. I'm glad you got that done, but let's keep right on going here.* I'm thinking, *Hey, wait a minute, I want to hear your verbal appreciation.* And so we have to define enough verbal appreciation. If I've done something for Bonnie, she'll say thank you, but on my Richter scale, her *thank you* is only a one or two. I want a major production and a granite monument—the John Lund Cleaned the Kitchen Monument. In other words, I want her to make a bigger deal out of it. So, how do we solve that? How about content communication and owning my expectation for appreciation in the present? How about not requiring Bonnie to remember that this is important to me? And finally, how about letting go of the dysfunctional value that if you have to ask it doesn't mean as much? I call Bonnie from whatever project she's working on and say, "Honey, can you take a break for a minute? It would mean a lot to me if you would come and make a big deal out of my cleaning the kitchen." This way, I'm owning the expectation—the expectation of appreciation.

Bonnie comes and takes my arm. I'm a touch-verbal, remember. So she takes my arm, and we tour the kitchen. I point out to her what a marvelous job I've done. She exclaims, "Oh, the hood! You cleaned the hood on the stove. Look at the floor! The floor is swept. Oh, that is so great." I add, "The floor was swept *and* mopped." Does it not count because I had to ask? It counts. Remember the great initiator-great responder rule. The other alternative is to feel unappreciated, pout, and say to myself, "That's the last time I go the extra mile." So we tour the kitchen. And sometimes I have to say, "Okay, that's enough oohing and aahing." Other times, I need more: "I did the pots and pans; they were really a mess tonight. See, they are down there. I cleaned them *all*."

This is how we own our expectations. There are things I do every day for Bonnie as an *I love you* in her love language for which I have no expectation of being rewarded. These are gifts with no strings attached. However, those things I do for which I would like special appreciation—like cleaning the kitchen, which was on her chore list, yes, I want those things to be acknowledged. We need to be able to say, "It would mean a lot to me if you would come over here and just sit next to me for a few minutes."

Our spouse may not always be able to meet our expectations, but I would rather be in the position of clearly communicating my expectations and having some of them rejected than the alternative—living in a world where I assume I'm not loved because this person isn't picking up on any of the indirect messages I'm sending her. It's better than my becoming a nagging, complaining person. It's totally unproductive to fill my mind and heart with resentment, wondering if I made a mistake in marrying because she really doesn't love me anyway. That kind of nonsense is all in my head, and it's the result of not owning my expectations and not being a content communicator.

Speak the Love Language of Those in Your Family

I often ask my students to try to speak the love language of those in their families for a week. They frequently discover that their children do not all speak the same love language. We often have some children who are very responsive to us, and it's likely they speak the same love language we do. All of my sons are strapping young men, and when I go to hug a couple of them, it's an emotionally painful experience for them. They tolerate it, but it is not something they enjoy. I'm not loving them in their love language as much as I am filling my own cup. But I also make special efforts to do things I know they will appreciate in their love languages. They know they cannot escape Dad's big hugs. They are thinking, *Are you done yet, Dad?* They're more like their mother; touch doesn't mean that much to them.

I would often ask my university students to live life as a visual person for one class period. I would ask them to act as if they had earmuffs on and duct tape their mouths. So, for one hour, they had to live with only their eyes. Now, granted, if you give a visual a mouth and an ear, it doesn't change their value system. It's still all about seeing things. We'll never change someone's inherent value system. I will never be as good a visual as Bonnie is, but I can let her know I love her by making an effort to speak her love language.

Bonnie and I love to travel the Middle East, and when we go to Egypt, I try to use the few words I know in Arabic. I attempt to communicate with the people. And just because I'm *willing* to speak a few words in their language, the Egyptians are impressed. And not only are they impressed, the men will throw their arms around me and give me a hug because I am trying to speak their language. I will never speak fluent Egyptian or Arabic, but I'll try. The point here is that it's important we make an attempt to speak the one another's love language.

For example, when Bonnie and I get up in the morning, Bonnie goes in to take a shower. While she's taking a shower, I make the bed. Now, I don't necessarily think that the bed needs to be made. I don't think the bed is lying there saying, "Okay, time to be made; I'm the bed. Your life will not be orderly unless you make me today. Last one out makes the bed." I don't think the bed cares, but Bonnie cares. In Bonnie's visual world, if she's in the kitchen and the bed isn't made, the world is in disarray. We need order. How can we have peace if there is not order?

I can live in total disarray and feel at peace. I'm serene and calm when there isn't any order, but I do make the bed as an *I love you* because it's important to Bonnie. Then when I go in a take a shower, Bonnie comes out and says, "You made the bed!" It's always a revelation to Bonnie, even after years of marriage. The idea here is that I can make an effort to communicate in Bonnie's love language, and she can try to communicate with me in touch-verbal ways. But even with that, it takes a conscious effort for me to remember that she's still in her visual world—when I come home, she's not hovering at the front door. She's doing things.

In the past, when we still had all eight children at home, Bonnie would stay up all night and work on projects, one night a week. There were no phone calls, no interruptions. And it caused a bit of friction when I said, "Honey, I would like you to come to bed. You know, together, just be with me." She'd be thinking, "But I can get so much accomplished." When it came to a work project, Bonnie would say, "You go and work in that room, I'll go work in this room, and we'll get twice as much done." Sometimes, not all the time, I didn't feel motivated to work alone. I wanted Bonnie to be in the same room as me—just *be* in the same room—even if we didn't talk. We didn't have to talk. I felt energized by just *being* with Bonnie.

That's how it is for some touch people. They need a certain amount of togetherness; for touch people, togetherness is a positive thing. So, how did we solve Bonnie's expectation of staying up all night working on a project versus my expectation of going to bed together? We negotiated as equals. I acknowledged that my expectation was not more important than her expectation. We came up with a going-to-bed ceremony. I'd say, "Honey, I'm going to bed." We'd have a word of prayer, talk for a few minutes, and just hold each other. Then we'd break. Ten or fifteen minutes at the most for the whole ceremony. I'd go to sleep or read scriptures for a few minutes. Bonnie was up and at 'em all night long. Had she done any good in the world today? Her value system would completely exhaust me. It takes conscious effort to try to discover and communicate in our mate's love language.

By the way, I did the same thing for the visuals in my university classes. We had everyone ear muffed and duct taped, and then we blindfolded them. The only thing they could do was use their hands. This helped verbals and visuals understand those of us who are touchy-feely.

I would ask students how they felt after these experiments, and they'd say, "I had no idea; it's a different world." We are all different. We can resent those differences or we can come to appreciate them. Mature love is when we appreciate those differences in our spouse. In reality, we can never have enough of our own love language. But we don't need to. We need to define what enough is going to be. We need to come up with concrete kinds of suggestions as to how we would feel appreciated, and then we need to decide what is enough verbal, visual, or touch. "This is what I would prefer . . ." "For me, that would mean the most . . ." Two of my favorite daily questions that help with understanding the needs of another person's love language are these:

1. What could I do for you today that would mean the most to you? I'm not always able to do it, but most of the time I can. I always add that I don't know if I can, but I'll make a special effort. Sometimes I'll arrange for a fix-it person to do what I can't, or Bonnie will say that it can be done later.

2. What is it that you are doing that I haven't appreciated or noticed as much as you would like? Remember, we will never be as good in the love language of our mates as they are. What is important is that we make the effort to communicate in their love language and to mutually define *enough!*

CHAPTER EIGHT

The Magnificent Seven

In order to understand some of the specific ways we can speak each other's love languages, we'll talk about what I call "The Magnificent Seven." If we did these seven things everyday, it would take us a total of forty-six minutes and one second.

The Magnificent Seven Love Language Behaviors

1. One verbal *I Love You* a day with eye contact
2. A five-second kiss
3. Ten seconds of verbal appreciation in person or on the phone
4. An hour date night once a week
5. A five-second hug
6. A twenty-five-second written expression
7. The fifteen-minute "Honey-do." (A talk, touch, or visual service of your mate's choosing. Or accumulate it to an hour and a half on Saturday. It is a gift of time given with a great attitude.)
8. Thirty total minutes of talk time—once in the morning, once at dinnertime, and once at bedtime.

The first of these magnificent seven is one verbal *I love you* a day, with eye contact. Now, what if we decided this *I love you* with eye contact was enough verbal appreciation for me and that if my spouse looks like she is not going to remember, I remind her. Reminding our spouse is not a sign of his or her failure; it is an expression of our need. Many people have made this a goal for the rest of their lives. Many of us do it naturally. One man came up to me and said, "When my wife tells me, 'I love you,' I feel like she's telling me I'm inadequate because she expects me to say, 'I love you' back, and so it's not that she loves me; she's trying to pull an *I love you* from me." That's not what this is about. I talked to him about both he and his wife becoming content communicators so his feelings of unspoken expectations could disappear. Again, it's important to be able to own our expectations, and it's okay to be a great responder. Let's not talk about our inadequacies and how we aren't good enough or how we don't measure up. Let's let it be enough for now. Let's simply say "I love you" every day, with eye contact.

One lady in my home ward was married for forty-nine years. She complained that her husband had always told her he loved her but that he never looked her in the eye when he said it. "I can't tell you what it means to me now, after forty-nine years of marriage, to have my husband look me in the eye and say he loves me." She was a visual. And so for her, these two messages were piggybacked—a verbal-visual, two-in-one *I love you.*

Number two of the magnificent seven is the five-second kiss. Talk about confirmation. After I read a book called *The 10-Second Kiss,* (Ellen Kreidman, PhD, Random House: New York, 1998), I talked Bonnie into trying it. I either caught her looking at her watch or she would start to giggle. So we changed the expectation to a five-second kiss. We could get through five seconds. Why a five-second kiss? The point is to share intimate space.

Number three of the magnificent seven is the ten-second expression of appreciation. This could be in person or on the phone, but sometime during the day, there's an expression of appreciation. There is a mind-set involved in this. We begin thinking of ways we can communicate acceptance, affection, and appreciation.

John Gottman tells us in his book *Why Marriages Succeed or Fail* that there needs to be a five-to-one ratio of positive to negative. If we don't achieve that ratio, the relationship will be headed on a collision course and eventually terminate. Gottman asserts that the reason relationships fail is because people do not put enough positives into their relationships. Relationships are like bank accounts. We have to make deposits if we are going to make withdrawals. So ten seconds of appreciation in person or on the phone counts. Saying, "Thank you for picking up my laundry. I appreciate it" makes a deposit in the emotional bank account.

Number four in the magnificent seven is the fifteen-minute "honey-do." For my honey-do from Bonnie, I want her to sit next to me, to hold my hand, to talk to me, to just be with me. Bonnie's a human *doing,* and I'm a human *being.* I want to be, and she wants to do. Talk is cheap with Bonnie. It's action Jackson. So Bonnie wants to save up her honey-do minutes and have me do a longer project for her on Saturday. Can we do this? Yes, we can. But we can only accumulate it for one week. So use it or lose it. I like my feet rubbed for fifteen minutes. I'll sit on the couch and watch the news while Bonnie rubs my feet. That's a very tactile thing. When Saturday comes around, I give her an hour and forty-five minutes on whatever work project she decides.

So you make a choice as to how you want to use your fifteen minutes. But remember to be adaptable. Be willing to try different things. I usually start my married children out with this program. I say, "I want you to do this for the first couple of months of your marriage and then kind of find out which ones work for you and perpetuate those."

Number five is the twenty-second hug. In the twenty-second hug, we obviously share space. This isn't a bear hug. We aren't talking about squeezing the life out of somebody. And we are not talking about a perfunctory hug. In order to help my students understand exactly what I'm talking about, I'll demonstrate this hug by having Bonnie assume a defensive posture as I initiate the hug. Her body language tells me she doesn't have time for more than a hug and that she's thinking I want more, but she has to get dinner and all kinds of things. That isn't very satisfying in a relationship. Next, we demonstrate a correct hug—a validating, twenty-second hug. Some may feel awkward about this—that it's contrived or phony. They feel like if we have to make an effort it's phony. That's not true. Whenever we make an effort to allow another person to feel more loved, it is not phony.

Number six is the twenty-five-second written expression. It doesn't have to be a Hallmark card everyday; that gets expensive. What I recommend is a spiral notebook or a phone-message pad. My daughter, who'd been married for three years, said, "Dad, I looked forward each day to seeing what my husband wrote as to why he appreciated me." She said, "I cannot tell you how important that was to me in our relationship and how much I looked forward to it."

What's nice about using a phone pad with duplicate sheets, is that you can tear the message out and give it to the person, and the copy is still in the book. Now, we should be careful not to think, "I'm going to write my note, and I'm going to wait and see how long it takes for her to notice it." If our partner is a visual, we're setting him or her up for failure unless he or she has it on their to-do list, palm pilot, etc. Touch and verbal people forget too. What I do is write the note. I always remember because I'm a verbal and it's important to me. I write the note, everyday, and put it on Bonnie's side of the bed with a pen. Then she comes in and remembers she needs to write. If she didn't notice, I say, "Honey, it would mean a lot to me if you would write in our appreciation book." Remember, if you have to ask, it *does* count.

Here is a bit of insanity. The touch person says, "I'll see how long she can go without a hug. I'm not going to hug her again until she initiates a hug!" Who is the one who suffers because there are no hugs? The visual? I doubt it. It is the touch person who is dying for want of physical affirmation. The insane thought is that the visual person is suffering for lack of hugs. The moral to the story is that some people want to punish their loved one in a love language that denies themselves the touch they desire. Bonnie would subconsciously be going on her merry way getting more things done. This is not how it should work.

We have to be careful not to use love language in a negative way. We think we can punish those we love in our own love language. Jim, a visual, says, "Well, if that's how she's going to be, I just won't do this and this for her." And Martha, a verbal person, is thinking, *I'll just give Jim the silent treatment.* And Jim is thinking, *Ah, peace and quiet and freedom. Beat me, beat me.* That's the insane part of it. We need to communicate in a positive way in our spouse's love language. We shouldn't make it hard for the other person to succeed; we shouldn't test them. We need to help them be successful with us. If we identify our expectations and not just wait for the other person to fail because they can't read our minds, we will feel more loved.

The last of the magnificent seven scares some people: Thirty minutes of talk time. However, it doesn't have to be all at once. It can be divided up into shorter segments: ten minutes when they get home, ten minutes around dinnertime, and ten minutes at bedtime. The idea is that for right now, it's enough. Let's define these seven magnificent behaviors as enough for now. We can make serious efforts to do these seven behaviors every day for a week or a month or for the rest of our lives if we want. We may have to get out of our comfort zones a bit, and practice all three love languages in the magnificent seven, and that is good. It will help you to become a more loving person. The magnificent seven encompass the verbal, the visual, and the touch in relation to sending and receiving messages of acceptance, affection, and appreciation. They make us feel like we are important and loved by another human being.

CHAPTER NINE

Content Communicating and Love Languages

Owning my love language and my specific needs by content communication got me in trouble. But I would rather deal with that trouble than live in a world of unmet expectations. At one point in our marriage, I'd made a habit of standing on the back landing when I came home and calling out for Bonnie. She'd be upstairs or downstairs, and I would say, "I'm here for a hug and a kiss." I didn't expect her to come to me. I would go to wherever she was. One particular day, Bonnie was in our kitchen talking with Mrs. Finley, Washington State supreme court justice's wife. She was the most sophisticated lady I will ever meet in my life. She must have taught Emily Post and Martha Stewart how to act. This was a lady who'd dress up to pull weeds. We were the large Mormon family next door.

Mrs. Finley was always having tea parties and backyard affairs. But this particular day, she happened to be in my kitchen talking to Bonnie to see if we'd take a pot roast off her hands since she and her husband had been called out of town at the last minute. They were at the top of the stairway when I came home all ready to ask for my hug and kiss, I could only see the back of Bonnie, and I thought she was talking to one of our kids. But Bonnie was in the middle of a discussion with Mrs. Finley. I was feeling really good, so I bounded up the stairs, singing at the top of my voice, "I'm home, I'm home, I'm home!" Bonnie started waving her hand behind her back in a gesture that meant, "Be quiet, stupid. Don't do what you are doing," but I didn't know that at the time. So I continued on up the stairs, and, when arrived, I was looking right into prim and proper Mrs. Finley's face as I said, "I'm here for a hug and kiss." I think Mrs. Finley was afraid she might get the hug and the kiss. This woman who always said the proper thing looked dumbfounded. The air was thick. Nobody knew what to say. Then Bonnie said two very profound things. The first thing she said was, "It's my husband." The second thing she said was, "He's home." That was enough to help Mrs. Finley regain her composure enough to excuse herself, and then she was out of there. But I'm thankful Bonnie was forgiving. I was simply owning my expectation for a hug and kiss of affection in my love language.

Let's not only be forgiving of our attempts at communicating, let's also take speaking each other's love language one step further. We need to talk about love languages in relation to content communication. Let's take the man who scored an 11 and a 9 in touch and visual. We'll call him Howard. Howard said, "I will show you how I love you by what I do for you, but I want to be validated by you touching me—by a hug or an arm around the shoulder, or holding my hand. That would mean a lot to me." His wife was a 14 verbal, and she was saying, "We don't ever talk." So Howard made a special effort to find time to talk, but what he discovered was that what he wanted to talk about and what she wanted to talk about were two different things. I told Howard that because verbal was his wife's love language, he needed to let her choose the agenda for the verbal time together. After all, she was willing to do things in his love language that were outside of her comfort zone. Howard agreed.

Nonsexual Touching

For me, touching is a wonderful thing because I am a 12-12-3. But we have to realize that if our partner is not a touching partner, they may assume that touching is going to end up in sexual intimacy. Touching can be foreplay or it can be an end in itself. How is anyone to know the difference? The answer lies in content communication. You can believe my words. Some touching is definitely sexual, so we leave that touching as off limits unless both parties verbally agree to it. This is why it's so important to have credibility. When you say what you mean and mean what you say, people can believe you.

Here is how a content communicator would deal with the issue of sexual intimacy. Let's say a man is talking to his wife, and that the man is a touch. He says, "Honey, I would like to feel free to give you a hug of affection several times during the day. I would like to be able to give you kisses of affection and hold your hand. All of this touching is an end in itself. It is not my intent to send you a signal that I want to have sexual intimacy. I don't want you to have to wonder. Let's agree right now that before we involve ourselves in anything sexual, we will have a clear verbal understanding of that. What this means is that you don't have to worry about my intent and touching. All touching will be nonsexual in nature, so don't try to read between the lines because there aren't any lines."

This next circumstance involved a woman who was a 19 touch married to a 19 visual. She said that she was dying for lack of feeling loved. The problem was that whenever she would want to hug or kiss or hold hands, her husband took it as a sign of her wanting to be sexual. It was her nature to be affectionate, and yet the only time he would touch her was to be sexual. His philosophy was, "Why touch if you are not going to do something about it?" So she felt like a prisoner. She couldn't touch him in public because he was embarrassed by displays of public affection. She couldn't give him a discrete hug without him interpreting it to mean something sexual.

When I met with this man, he confirmed that he saw all touching as having sexual meaning. I challenged him to change his paradigm or risk losing his wife. It was an adjustment he was willing to make, but it was awkward because he was raised in a family where there was no public display of affection, not ever. He said that he had never seen his father and mother kiss or hold hands. He said that he could not remember being hugged or kissed by his mother or father and he couldn't remember any of his brothers or sisters being hugged or kissed, either. It didn't take long for this man to overcome his family's nontouching tradition. He committed to implement the magnificent seven touch, verbal, and visual behaviors on a daily basis. He and his wife agreed that all touching would be an end in itself and that sexual intimacy would be verbally agreed upon. To launch them forth, I asked them how many times a week they were comfortable having sexual intimacy. They agreed upon twice a week. I was very specific and asked them to choose for the next three months which two days of the week that would be. Tuesdays and Saturdays were the designated days. The reason for being this explicit was so that they could practice being affectionate independent of the expectations of anything sexual. The results were miraculous. His wife was freed from her prison of nontouching, and he found a great deal of satisfaction in being exposed to a new universe of touching without being sexual.

All of these stories and a hundred more are testimonies of couples needing to discuss touching, especially a touching person with a nontouching person. It needs to be clear that when we do touch, it is an end in itself and not a message that there is something else going on. If touching people want hugs and such, we need to communicate that touching is about affection, not sexual intimacy. It has been helpful for touching and nontouching people to agree that sexual intimacy will not occur unless there is a prior verbal agreement with this understanding. Nontouching people feel freer to allow appropriate nonsexual touching. It can be an end in itself.

Meeting Verbal Needs

What about the love language of verbals? Most of the verbals I know say that they have to talk to their mothers or friends or sisters or, if they're a man, other men. However, there aren't as many men verbals as women. But there has to be someone else besides their spouse to fill that verbal cup. They *have* to talk to people. However, if a verbal needs to share with someone other than their spouse, let's make sure that other person is someone *both* spouses feel good about, especially if the spouse is going to be discussed in anything but generic terms. Otherwise the verbal person can talk to everyone in the universe. Even though men are really private, when we remember that the average woman uses twenty-one thousand communication signals per day and that the average man uses seven thousand, most men don't want to be responsible for the remaining fourteen thousand communication signals the average woman is going to want to share. With that thought in mind, finding a "safe" third party both of them can agree upon seems like a reasonable alternative. That sister-in-law or sister or the wife's lady-friend is looking better all the time as candidates to share his wife's fourteen thousand words. I recommend that the couple agree on a safe third party, even fourth and fifth party, that the verbal person can talk to about sensitive things so the expectation of the verbal person is not all placed on just one person (the spouse). Of course, the verbal person is free to talk to everybody else for as long she wants as long as she doesn't talk about sensitive things her husband would consider a violation of trust.

As we discussed previously, women universally want more information from men than men are willing to give. One of the great challenges we face in interacting is this male-female difference. Men generally don't enjoy bonding by sharing verbally. They prefer to bond by doing things together. One of the reasons men are reluctant to share themselves with women is that they don't trust women. They are afraid that women are going to go tell everybody everything about their personal lives. When a man opens up and shares something, he figures his mother-in-law and all his sisters and everyone else is going to know everything he shares with his wife.

This creates somewhat of a dilemma when the wife says, "I want you to open up and share." The guy's thinking, *Yeah, right. It will be on the evening news.* So, if the woman feels a need to bond through sharing verbally, the solution is to have some safe people in her life, people she and her husband both designate for sharing. There are people in my wife's family you could tell almost anything because they are safe for me. They're going to love me no matter what you tell them, so I don't mind if she shares with them. If she respects that boundary, I'm going to be more inclined to share with her. But if she's a loose cannon, I feel like I can't have confidence in her.

When there's someone who's reluctant to share, maybe it's because they don't trust you, but we must also consider the reality that for men, sharing often involves exposing fears and doubts. Men tend to interpret sharing those kinds of things as a sign of weakness. They don't realize that women perceive men's hopes, dreams, and fears as positive things. When women express their frustrations, it's a real mental release for them. Men tend to store things, and they usually don't process information the same way. So it may be a great mental and emotional release for a woman, but sharing does not have the same effect for most men.

For several years, I've served on the Utah Commission on Marriage. A member of the Church's Relief Society general presidency also attends these meetings. I remember a conversation I had with the president of this organization. I asked her what she had learned in her interactions with men and women, and her response was this: "Well, I've learned that a man needs a woman, and a woman needs a man *and* other women she can talk to." Fifty percent of men have no one other than their wife as an intimate in terms of communication. Forty percent of men will have one other person—a brother, a father, a friend—somebody they would consider an intimate. Even with that one person, they don't necessarily share everything. They are very cautious about sharing information. Only 10 percent of men have multiple friendships that are considered intimates.

Most women would starve to death if that was all they had. Women need to have others with whom they can share. Men don't necessarily bond by sharing. They bond by sharing space and feeling accepted. Men can sit in a fishing boat, for example, for a couple of hours and feel bonded at the end of that experience, and they may have not said a word the entire time. They'll play a game of basketball, run up and down the court, knock each other over, and feel really bonded by that experience, not having said much of anything.

Women tend to bond by sharing verbally. So even though it may be hard for them, men should make special efforts to share what they feel they can and at the least be better at listening to their wives. Men can bond with their wives by listening to them. One of the dilemmas with this, however, is that to a man, a woman's "sharing" sometimes comes across as complaining, and when a man hears a woman complaining, he assumes that it's somehow his responsibility to fix the situation, which is not true most of the time.

Visuals and Love Language

Visuals usually need to cut their list of expectations in half, not only their expectations of other people but also of themselves. Otherwise, they set themselves up for a lot of frustration by way of their unmet expectations. Visuals are best reminded that an elephant can be eaten one bite at a time. It means elephant steaks, elephant sausages, elephant burgers, and elephant stew. Nonvisuals already feel they can never do enough to please the visual since it is the visual's expectation to eat the whole elephant and have others take their fair share of the responsibility to eat it also. It behooves the visual to present his or her requests for productive behaviors in reasonable bites and to remember to define *enough* in terms that are acceptable to nonvisuals. Otherwise, the nonvisual will simply avoid the visual as an impossible-to-please elephant eater. Remember, if the nonvisual person gives everything and the visual is still going to be unhappy, the nonvisual will wonder why he or she should give anything because the visual won't be happy no matter what. The nonvisual may determine that if only one person in the relationship is going to be happy, it might as well be himself. All the love languages include impossible-to-please people. Visuals, however, are prone to be perceived as impossible to please, even if they are not. Because of this perception I keep encouraging the visual to define what is enough for this week or today or for the next four hours.

Another important point for visuals to consider is the importance of getting other people to help them with the tasks that seem so important to them rather than putting all of the burden on their nonvisual family members. The visual man who expects his nonvisual wife to keep the house immaculate may find it in his best interest to hire out some of the housework rather than alienate his wife. "Enough" would be to concur that she keeps three agreed-upon rooms clean to a certain level; the housekeeper does the rest. Or they can do a "walk through" of each room and agree to a certain level of cleanliness. Then, if the visual man wants to do more, he can. They must also have the understanding that his cleaning to a higher standard is not a sign of her inadequacy but a product of his personal expectations. She can become a cheerleader and say as he is cleaning, "Go, hubby, go!"

In order for visuals to take care of all the things they see need to be done, they need to be able to consider alternative ways of getting those things done—get children to do some of the work, hire plumbers, electricians, yard work professionals, etc. Since it's impossible for visuals to get everything they perceive as important accomplished by themselves, they may have to realize that the universe is not going to fall in line with their expectations. If they do not find alternative ways of having their expectations met, they run the risk of becoming toxic people. They may also find that their unmet expectations have turned them into someone even they don't like.

Male or female visuals often perceive the things they provide as an extension of themselves. This means that if the house, the car, or the gifts they provide or care for are not kept in good condition, they feel they are not appreciated.

On the bright side, visuals are doers. Therefore, they need to add to their lists the Magnificent Seven Love Language Behaviors.

Just because we've been married a long time doesn't mean we understand our mate's love language. A person may work hard to show their spouse they love them, but if the spouse speaks a different love language, there will be mutual frustration. Take Tevye in *Fiddler on the Roof* for example. Twenty-five years into their marriage, he asks Golde if she loves him. And she says something like, "What do you mean, do I love you? I cook your food, I've had your children, and I've done this and this and this. Look at all of the things I've done." Golde's obviously a visual. "Just open your eyes and look, and you can see." Then she has to stop and ask herself, "Do I love him?" And she answers herself, "I suppose I do."

Making the Effort

What happens when we truly make a conscious effort to communicate in our mate's love language? First and foremost, our efforts are appreciated. It's the Egyptians all over again. They come up, put their arms around us, and say thank you. "Thank you for trying to communicate with us." Even when I slaughter a word, they'll laugh and say, "No, it's pronounced this way." I'll ask, "What did I say?" And they respond, "You just said you're a big goat." I didn't mean that, but in the end, they know I've tried to speak their language, and that goes a long way. The same goes for trying to speak our mate's love language.

By defining "enough" in any of the love languages (touch, verbal, or visual), we are preparing to be successful. We are setting ourselves and our spouses up for success. In redefining our expectations, we are reducing our own frustrations. The ultimate objective is to become more loving. Doing the things discussed in these chapters will contribute to you becoming a more loving person.

CHAPTER TEN

Articles of Commitment

In order for love to flourish and for a relationship to prosper, the negative needs to be managed. Unresolved conflicts are like the coals of a fire resting on the ground of a beautiful forest. If the coals are left unattended, they will eventually be fanned by the winds of criticism and erupt into a blazing forest fire that destroys everything beautiful which once surrounded it.

The most important relationship any one of us will ever have or have had in all eternity is with our Heavenly Father. He has a plan to deal with the negative in our lives. It is a perfect plan because its ultimate objective is for each of us to become our highest and best self. It is founded in God's love for us. It was anticipated that we'd have a considerable amount of negative in our lives. But God's plan included a way out of the negative. We may call it repentance and forgiveness, but it is a plan to manage and eventually eliminate the negative from our lives.

It would not be wrong to suggest that the husband-wife relationship requires a similar plan to manage the negative, that the plan be based in love and have as its objective both members becoming their highest and best selves. The plan should include a way out of the negative and a way to eventually eliminate it or at least minimize it.

The plan needs to be flexible enough to deal with the different personalities involved. It has to be consistent with the revealed principles of the gospel—harmony with the scriptures and the teachings of the living prophet. Does such a plan exist? The answer is yes. There is power in every righteous covenant. If one person honors his or her covenants, even if the spouse doesn't, there are divine promises that come into play on his or her behalf. The Lord will find a way to not only edify the covenant-keeper but also influence for good those with whom he or she comes in contact.

The plan is simple: increase your skills to love others and decrease the toxic behavior that makes it difficult for others to love you. This is not about you trying to change your mate. It is about two people becoming one. It is about you taking responsibility for those things over which you have control.

Now that we have a basic understanding about the appropriate use of love languages, we are going to talk about managing the negative. We are going to explore how to deal with negative conflicts in healthy ways. It's okay to have differences of opinion. It's not okay to have contention. Contention is different from conflicting opinions. Ultimately, we will learn how to resolve our differences so that we can agree to disagree without becoming disagreeable, or toxic.

So, what can we do when a spouse isn't willing to do what we want them to? Remember, marriage is a relationship of equals. We must speak the language of equals and learn how to negotiate in a relationship of equals. This can only happen as we agree to abide by correct principles. Again, we will never carry out the Lord's program in the devil's way. How we deal with the negative in our life must be grounded in principles of love, gentleness, patience, and long-suffering. By doing so we will invite the powers of heaven to divinely intervene and to do what we cannot accomplish without them.

Read the following "Ten Articles of Commitment to Myself and to My Mate." Ask yourself if you are willing to focus ninety days of your life on becoming your highest and best self.

Becoming a More Loving Person

Ten Articles of Commitment to Myself and to My Mate

ARTICLE I

I am willing to learn to become a more loving person. I am willing to sincerely commit myself to keeping my mind and heart open to the information, knowledge, and skills that I will receive. I will practice the skills I have learned or will yet learn to improve my ability to communicate loving behaviors. [You are agreeing to be teachable and to put into practice some of the new skills to which you will be exposed.]

ARTICLE II

I am willing to pay a price in time and emotional energy in order to increase my knowledge and skills. I am willing to reprioritize my schedule to make time to implement these behaviors. [You are agreeing to make time in your existing schedule to increase your knowledge and to reprioritize your schedule if necessary, so you can make time to learn how to become more loving.]

ARTICLE III

I am willing to become a content communicator. I will own my words and be responsible for the verbal content of my messages. I will say what I mean and mean what I say. I will avoid hint dropping and relying upon body language or nonverbal means of communicating. I will not expect others to read my mind or discern the intent of my expectations. I will own my words in a respectful manner. I will not parent my equals by suggesting what they should, need, and ought to do. [This is a commitment to be a content communicator.]

ARTICLE IV

I am willing to work on a positive attitude. I am willing to admit there are areas of strength as well as areas of weakness in my ability to communicate love. I am willing to maximize my loving behaviors and work on eliminating the toxic traits that make me less lovable and to focus on those skills that will enhance positive points of contact between myself and others. [This commitment is about having a positive attitude and working on developing both loving behaviors and eliminating the toxic traits that keep us from being more loving.]

ARTICLE V

I am willing to commit to a sincere effort to improve my communications skills in my mate's love language and to be a greater source of affection, acceptance, and appreciation. [This is about learning to value other peoples' love languages as well as learning to define your own. It includes the Magnificent Seven Love Language Behaviors.]

ARTICLE VI

I am willing to refrain from speaking ill of my mate to friends, family, or strangers. I will not embarrass or belittle my mate in front of others by making critical comments, nor will I be critical of my mate in their absence. I will also ask for permission to criticize my mate. [Here, you are going to try to manage your own critical nature. You are asked to go twenty-four hours without criticizing. Don't be discouraged if it takes you weeks to achieve one period of twenty-four consecutive hours of not being critical. I have had policemen and IRS agents complete this task. You can do it.]

ARTICLE VII

I am willing to forgive my mate for all past wrongs, hurt feelings, unmet expectations, and personal heartache, and to let God be the judge. I will also forgive myself for personal failures and rededicate myself to becoming my highest and most loving self. [This is about freeing yourself from the past and not letting your tomorrows be held hostage by your yesterdays.]

ARTICLE VIII

I am willing to focus on becoming my highest and best self. I am 100 percent responsible for my expectations and my half of any relationship to which I am a party. I will seek to become the best I can be. I will not focus on fear and doubt in spite of any feelings of personal inadequacy or past failures. [In this article, you are agreeing to accept responsibility for your own happiness and not transfer your ability to be of good cheer to anyone else.]

ARTICLE IX

I am willing to set aside any conflicting relationships in order to devote myself to properly focusing on my ability to love my mate. [If there are any third-party conflicting relationships that may include friends, parents, former lovers or current ones, you will set them aside and focus with honor and integrity 100 percent effort on the relationship you are trying to improve.]

ARTICLE X

I am willing to work on these assignments for ninety consecutive days. If I miss a day I will rededicate myself to sincere effort until I have achieved a total of ninety days.

[You will make a serious effort to complete ninety days of being true to all ten articles. They do not have to be consecutive days. It may take you one hundred and fifty days to complete ninety, but you are committing to make the effort. Both partners are to sign this agreement.]

Signature_____

Date to Begin_____

Signature_____

Date to Begin_____

[*This is a way of formalizing the commitment. It also gives you a beginning date and ninety days later an exit. I have personally taken this pledge and I can offer my humble witness that you will become a more loving person as you complete it.*]

Once you have signed the above personal commitment with honesty, you are prepared for an incredible journey of the human spirit—the adventure of becoming a more loving person. There are no guarantees that others will love you just because you are more loving person. However, not being loving does make you less attractive to those about whom you care. A second set of unattractive traits called "toxic behaviors" will be dealt with later. Eliminating toxic behaviors and becoming a more loving person are keys to being loved. The human spirit is attracted to love and is repelled by nonacceptance messages. It's really a simple plan: Increase your skills to love others and decrease the toxic behaviors that make it difficult for others to love you.

This is a commitment you can keep if you are single, engaged, or married. If you are single, pick a roommate or family member as a focus of these commitments. Obviously, an engaged or married couple will have each other as the focus of their commitment. This is not a promise to be perfect. It's a commitment of willingness. It is really a contract with yourself. There are no punishments, and there are no penalties except the ones we bring on ourselves by the poor choices we make. You have nothing to lose, and you have a more loving you to encounter at the end of ninety successful days.

Goals Versus Wishes

There are only two choices you have in life. You can choose how you want to act toward others, and you can choose how you are going to react when you are the victim of the poor choices of others. One wise man observed, "It is easier to act like a Christian than to react like one." It is easier to take a casserole to a sick neighbor than it is to react nicely to the same neighbor who yelled at your children to get off his lawn.

You cannot become your best self by trying to control or manipulate others. For the next ninety days, focus on the two choices you have. Let go of what others should do or be and devote yourself to taking control over your half of any relationship.

Remember, conflict stems from unmet expectations. It is helpful to examine our expectations to see which ones we can control and which ones depend upon others and over which we have no control.

We might think of a goal as something that depends on us and a wish as something that requires someone else to perform in a certain way. We might ask ourselves how much of our life is goal-oriented and how much of it is wish-oriented. "I'll be happy when everyone I love does everything I want the way I want it done." That, of course, is not a goal because we have no control over others. It is a huge, monstrous wish. If we were to sit down and look at our expectations, how many of those expectations are wishes and how many are goals? For example, if I were a young married student I might say it's my wish to get all A's in my classes. It couldn't be a goal because of the subjectivity of the teachers who give the grades. However, I could set a goal to study for four hours each day. I could have a goal of turning in all my homework, of getting up every morning at 6:30 AM, of exercising for thirty minutes a day, of having my personal prayers, of having personal scripture study for twenty minutes, of attending all my classes on days I am healthy, and of taking notes in all my classes.

What you can't set as a goal is what your spouse may or may not do. "We will . . ." statements are not goals; they are wishes. It would be appropriate to say, "I will invite my spouse to pray with me on a daily basis." That is an achievable goal which depends upon you. It is a "wish" to say my spouse and I are going to have daily prayer together. Let's say you have a "goal" to pray together every day as a couple, and yet it doesn't happen. You are now frustrated and begin to nag your husband to pray with you, and you begin to be critical of him for not praying. He is keeping you from your righteous "goal," which of course, is actually a wish. You become a person you don't like. You find yourself more and more resentful of him and more fault-finding. Why? Because your expectation of joint prayer is not being met.

Now let's change the paradigm. Your expectation is that you will invite him to pray daily with you. If he comes one or two days a week, you say to him, "Thank you for praying with me. It means a lot to me." You are successful because your expectation was something over which you had control.

Make a list of either your frustrations or a list of your expectations. Place an asterisk by either your frustrations or your expectations that are "goals" and a circle by those that are "wishes." Now, how can you rewrite your expectations as a goal to which you can contribute?

°Wish	*Goal
°Couple Prayer	*I will be available for couple prayer, and I will invite my spouse to pray with me everyday in a kind way.
	*Personal Prayer

In the above example, we are going to rewrite the expectation from a goal over which you have control. The expectation of couple prayer is changed to "I will be available everyday for couple prayer and I will invite my spouse to pray with me in a kind way every day." By changing your expectations to achievable goals, you are removing a great deal of frustration from your life.

The extent to which we require "wishes" to be met before we can feel good and be happy is the same extent to which we are setting ourselves up for frustration and unhappiness. As Mary, the sister of Martha, washed the feet of Jesus with her hair and anointed Him with precious spikenard from the alabaster box, she was criticized by Judas Iscariot (John 12:1–6). Simon, the cured leper, who was also the father of Judas Iscariot, considered Mary a sinner. Jesus rebuked both Judas and Simon. "Let her alone" (Mark 14:6), . . . "Her sins, which are many, are forgiven; for she loved much" (Luke 7:47), and "She hath done what she could" (Mark 14:8). Obviously, Jesus does not expect us to control things over which we have no power. We cannot control others. What he does expect is that we love much and do what we can. If our goals are consistent with this standard, we can be of good cheer regardless of whether or not all our loved ones are doing everything we would like them to do.

How much of our lives are dependent on things over which we have no control? It might save us a lot of unnecessary frustration if we take a look at our "goals." Even if our expectations are reasonable and realistic, they may not work if they require other people to follow through. If we make it an expectation that we will only be happy when everybody does what we want them to do, in the way we want it done, we may end up becoming a control freak, a micro-manager, feeling a need to enforce our expectations. That's a difficult place to be. From a scriptural point of view, it is hell. The Book of Mormon prophet Samuel defined frustration perfectly: "For ye have sought all the days of your lives for that which ye could not obtain" (Helaman 13:38).

There are certain things, however, over which we do have control. In a previous chapter, we talked about the challenge to refrain from criticism for twenty-four hours. I issue this challenge to my students to help them to see whether they've become overly critical of others, whether they have the "Eeyore Syndrome" (the donkey in the *Winnie the Pooh* series): "It's probably going to rain today." "They're not going to like me at work." The good news is that no one is born a pessimist; we are taught those kinds of behaviors in our family constructs. We can, with some effort, replace those behaviors and attitudes with healthier ones.

I now reissue the challenge to you. Go for twenty-four hours without criticizing anyone for anything, including yourself. You may want to purchase a notebook or a journal in which you can write down your thoughts and feelings about your progress on this and other challenges you will accept as we progress on our journey of becoming a more loving you. The rules are simple. Don't criticize. When you do make a critical statement, start your twenty-four hours over. If a critical thought enters your mind and you are able to dismiss it in less than thirty seconds, you don't need to start over. We can practice these skills in our family home evenings, and if we make a mistake, as we know we will, we place a nickel in a jar. Then when it gets to a certain point, we go and buy something fun for the whole family.

President Harold B. Lee once said that you cannot live in the world and not be faced with evil thoughts. He went on to say that having an evil thought does not make you evil. However, he explained, if you choose to dwell upon that thought, you are choosing an evil course. He continued to share that he has memorized several long poems and a number of Church hymns, and when he is faced with an evil thought he repeats in his mind the words to the poems or hymns until he is in control of his thoughts. Sometimes, he said, it takes several verses (author's personal interview with Harold B. Lee, September 1965).

Criticism is as much a habit as anything. But we must learn to overcome such a habit. As it says in Doctrine and Covenants 88:124, "Cease to find fault one with another." President Thomas S. Monson often quotes the verses of the LDS hymn, "Let Us Oft Speak Kind Words," and for forty years he's encouraged the members of the Church to have a positive outlook toward life and to share loving words one with another. His fervent testimony included this charge: "There are hearts to gladden. There are kind words to say" (Thomas S. Monson, Conference Report, October 1965, 143). We must learn to contain ourselves. President Gordon B. Hinckley, in a talk he had given three different times because he felt so strongly about it, said,

> What a wonderful time to be alive. How enthusiastic I feel. . . . I hope that you are enthusiastic, because there is a terrible ailment of pessimism in the land. It's almost endemic. We're constantly fed a steady and sour diet of character assassination, faultfinding, evil speaking of one another. . . . The tragedy is that this spirit of negativism seems to prevail throughout the country. . . .
>
> This spirit has infected the atmosphere on university campuses and the workplace, even this campus. The snide remark, the sarcastic gibe, the cutting down of associates—these too often are the essence of our conversation. In our homes, wives weep and children finally give up under the barrage of criticism leveled by husbands and fathers. Criticism is the forerunner of divorce, the cultivator of rebellion, sometimes a catalyst that leads to failure. Even in the Church it sows seeds of inactivity and, finally, in many cases, apostasy.

I come this evening with a plea that we stop seeking out the storms and enjoy more fully the sunlight. ("The Lord is at the Helm," BYU Fireside, Sunday, 6 March 1994)

This was a prophet of God, a prophet for the latter-days, our days. And he said that there is a terrible ailment in the land and that it has affected the minds and hearts of almost everybody everywhere. It's so much a part of us that we're not even aware of it much of the time. If we had lived in Sodom and Gomorrah, would we have been aware of what was going on or would we have just been part of the culture, oblivious to the signs of the times? In the same talk, President Hinckley asked of us, "I come . . . with a plea that we stop seeking out the storms and enjoy more fully the sunlight. I'm suggesting that we accentuate the positive."

That's why we talk about love language. It's important to build on the positives in our relationships. No relationship is going to survive if we pick at each other's faults and shortcomings. According to President Hinckley, there isn't a relationship around that can survive such negativism:

I'm asking that we look a little deeper for the good, that we still our voices of insult and sarcasm, that we more generously compliment virtue and effort. I'm not asking that all criticism be silent. . . .

I'm not suggesting that our conversation be all honey. . . . What I am suggesting and asking is that we turn from the negativism that so permeates our society and look for the remarkable good in the land and times in which we live, that we speak of one another's virtues more than we speak of one another's faults, that optimism replace pessimism.

It's interesting to me that there are no real pessimists. If we talk to a pessimist, they aren't really pessimists; they are realists. In their minds, pessimists are realists. But there is a danger in thinking, *I'm sure you're talking about someone else.* We must take ownership, and we must let faith replace our fears.

In each one of us there lives a pack of wolves—wolves of passion, wolves of fear and doubt, even wolves of faith and love, and yet, interestingly enough, in every wolf pack, only one wolf dominates. It is known as the alpha wolf. The other wolves in the pack will be subservient to the alpha wolf. What is the alpha wolf of our life? Is it fear? Doubt? Insecurity? Or is it faith? Hope? Optimism?

Certainly, the alpha wolf in our life is the one we feed. If we feed fear, fear will be the alpha wolf. Love can be the alpha wolf in a relationship, but if we feed a relationship with criticism and negativism, then negativism becomes the alpha wolf that dominates the relationship.

Remember, relationships are like bank accounts: we have to make deposits if we plan on making withdrawals. It's not that there isn't a time for appropriate criticism. It's just that we need to learn *how* to do it so we don't deplete each other's bank accounts. Dr. Gottman asserts that the number-one reason relationships fail stems from the inability to resolve conflict in healthy ways. President Hinckley said we must let our faith replace our fears. He went on to say,

> My father often said to us, "Cynics do not contribute, skeptics do not create, doubters do not achieve." . . . There is too much fruit-less, carping criticism. . . . In our individual circumstances let us look for and cultivate the wonders of our opportunities. . . . It is so easy, under the pressure of the daily grind, to become negative and critical, to be shortsighted, and even go down in defeat. . . . On one occasion when the Savior was walking among a crowd, a woman who had been long sick touched his garment. He perceived that strength had gone out of him. The strength that was his had strengthened her. So may it be with each of us. Let me urge you to desist from making cutting remarks one to another.

Unfortunately, some of us were raised in families that could not complete a sentence without sarcasm. President Hinckley observed, "Clever expression that is sincere and honest is a skill to be sought and cultivated" (ibid). Being witty and able to share a "clever expression" is different than "the snide remark, the sarcastic gibe, the cutting down of associates" warned against by President Hinckley (ibid). To be witty is not what he is talking about here. He thinks that being witty and being able to turn a phrase into a "clever expression" is a delightful thing. However, if someone suffers because of what we are saying and they are made, in any way, to look less than what they are, then that is an inappropriate criticism and a "clever expression" of which we should not partake.

There's a difference between being witty and tearing someone down. The word *sarcasm* actually comes from a Greek word "sarkazein" meaning "to tear flesh." And some of us have that as a style of communicating. Maybe we call it a pun or a play on words, but if someone is going to hurt because of it, if we are going to strip a little flesh, then it becomes sarcasm we need to leave alone. A great rule of thumb is Doctrine and Covenants 50:23, "And that which doth not edify is not of God." In 1846, Thomas Carlyle said, "Sarcasm, I now see to be, in general, the language of the Devil, for which reason I have long since as good as renounced it" (Crystal, David and Hilary. "Unfriendly Language," *Words on Words,* Chicago: University of Chicago Press, 2000, 174).

President Hinckley went on to urge each of us to "desist from the cutting remarks one to another, rather cultivate the art of complimenting, the art of strengthening, the art of encouraging. It is an art to encourage and to strengthen. As members of the Church, each one of us has been divinely commissioned to bear one another's burdens, to strengthen one another, to lift one another, to look for the good in one another, and to emphasize that good" (ibid).

As President Hinckley so eloquently pointed out, there is power in looking for the good:

> There is not a man or a woman in this vast assembly who cannot be depressed on the one hand or lifted on the other by the remarks of his or her associates. . . . All of this seems to say to me every one . . . might have done much better . . . had he received less of criticism and more of encouragement.
>
> My dear young friends don't partake of the spirit of our times. Look for the good and build on it. There is so much of the sweet and the decent and the good to build upon.
>
> You are partakers of the gospel of Jesus Christ. The gospel means "good news." The message of the Lord is one of hope and salvation. The voice of the Lord is the voice of gladness, the work of the Lord is the work of glorious and certain reward. I do not suggest that you simply put on rose-colored glasses to make the world look rosy. I ask rather that you look above and beyond the negative, the critical, the cynical, the doubtful, to the positive. (President Gordon B. Hinckley, Fireside, BYU Marriott Center, Sunday, March 6, 1994)

Permission to Criticize

There are currently thirty-eight scriptures that encourage us to cease finding fault with one another. If we are going to do things differently than we've been used to out in the world, if we're going to practice a higher law, we need to rethink how we go about criticism.

As we mentioned before, there's a better way when it comes to criticism. This is what containment is about. If I want to say something critical to my children, for example, I give them an option. I say, "I need to talk to you; I have some criticism, and I need to share it with you. Can I talk to you now, or should I talk to you later?" I am not giving them a choice as to whether or not they *get* to hear my criticism, only whether they want to hear it now or later. I will say to my daughter, Kaari, for example, "Kaari, I have something I need to share with you; it is critical. We can do it now, or we can do it later. So, let me know." And she will sometimes say, "Oh, Dad, I don't want to know later. I want to know right now. You are going to ruin my whole night unless you tell me. Please, as painful as it is, tell me now." My youngest son, Joseph, has a different approach: "Let's wait until later, Dad." Joseph is hoping I'll forget. I'm not going to forget, but I will make it later. I can do this when it's about communicating and not about anger.

Remember that, unlike with a child, in a relationship of equals with our spouse or our adult children, we can't just say, "You should, you need, you ought." The reality is that once we kneel at the altar or we've made the vows of marriage, we've driven each other off the used-car lot. And there's a big sign in the window—"As is." We pretty well take that person as is. We don't take back our used car and ask the salesman to fix this and fix that and make all these repairs. We bought it "As is." We are not our spouse's coach; we are his or her cheerleader. If I have a criticism I want to share with Bonnie, what gives me the authority to share that criticism is not my frustration but her permission. In other words, in sharing criticism with an equal, we need their permission.

If I say to Bonnie, "I have something I'd like to share with you, and it is critical. I hoped that you would find a few minutes so I could share it with you," and she says, "I'm preparing a lesson, and now would be a bad time. I don't need any negative thoughts while I'm trying to be spiritual. So, no, now is not a good time," then I respect her decision. Our tendency is to feel like we've got a mouth and a thought. We want to say it, and we think Bonnie should hear it right now because we've been addicted to criticizing whenever we want to.

Everything we do to detract from the message makes us less effective as communicators. And conversely, whatever we do to keep the focus on the message makes us more effective communicators. We practice a lot of self-defeating behaviors that make us less effective in communicating things that are important. Some of us feel that the Lord has appointed us to make observations about everyone's life. We feel it's our mission to be the super critic. Some of us actually feel it's our right to do that. But we don't have the right. Anything we do that detracts from the message—if we're out of control and screaming or yelling—puts the focus not on the message but on our being emotionally out of control. But if we ask for permission to criticize our mate, and they give us permission, it's going to keep the focus on the message.

We must decide we want to be effective in our communication, and that it's not just because we're angry and want to vent about how unhappy and miserable we are. That's called complaining, and complaining is something children, not equals, do. A complaining person will feel like they're a child in a relationship because they feel powerless. "I'm a child so I might as well complain about the circumstances." They don't feel like they have any control over the situation.

So how do we ensure that both partners feel like equals? First of all, we must realize that there is no such thing as constructive criticism. That is an oxymoron. J. Golden Kimball made this astute observation: "There are weasel words out there. Do you know what a weasel does? Well it will bite an end of an egg, sucks everything out of it, and leaves nothing but the shell. Some people speak that way. They use weasel words. One word takes all the meaning out of the other" (Lund, John L. *The Art of Giving and Receiving Criticism,* Salt Lake City: The Communications, 1997, 47).

Constructive criticism is a weasel expression; one word takes the meaning out of the other. Here's a weasel expression—"He is a wise fool." How about this one: "I'm going to ride the up-down elevator." "Which one?" we might ask. "Well, both at the same time. I'm going to go up and down at the same time." We can see the insanity of such thought, but then we think we can constructively criticize someone.

To criticize is to tear down. To construct is to build up. It's a lot like remodeling. Remodeling involves two different processes, a tearing down and a building up. We can't do both at the same time. We can tear something down and then we can replace it, but that is not "constructive" criticism because criticism only tears down. When a well-meaning person shares "constructive criticism," he is sending in the wrecking crew. Except for its redundancy, "destructive criticism" is a more accurate phrase to describe the tearing-down process. The constructive process is an edifying one, a building up. Positive reinforcement best describes the construction process.

There is necessary and appropriate criticism, but it's never constructive. Criticism is always about tearing something down. Some things need to be torn down. However, it must be done in a way consistent with the gospel of Jesus Christ. Criticism is a toxic substance, and, like all toxic substances, it should be kept in a special container. Therefore, we need to be able to contain criticism. As President Hinckley pointed out, we live in a time when there is a spirit of "negativism that permeates our society"(*Ensign,* April 1986, 2). Containment involves restraint, but it is not external restraint that President Hinckley references. It is self-restraint based on respecting another person enough that we ask for his or her permission before we offer criticism. President Hinckley invited us to develop the "art of complimenting, of strengthening, of encouraging." In that same spirit, we can develop the art of giving appropriate criticism and the art of receiving appropriate criticism in the Lord's way.

CHAPTER ELEVEN

The Art of Giving Criticism

Once we understand the importance of receiving permission to criticize, we must learn that there is an art to giving criticism. If we're going to learn any art, there are certain things we must do. Remember, Dr. John Gottman reasons that relationships fail because of our inability to resolve conflicts in healthy ways. We are going to talk about these healthy ways. Dr. Gottman also said that relationships fail because people lack willingness, skills, or knowledge. It is almost certain that unwillingness will defeat every solution.

Let's look at some scripturally-based principles that relate to the art of giving criticism. First, before we offer any criticism, it's important we ask ourselves two questions: "Is the criticism part of my stewardship or is it my business?" If not, it's probably something we should keep to ourselves. Second, we must ask ourselves, "Is the criticism not only true, but is it also necessary?" If we *constantly* criticize and tell others what we think, we are going to destroy our effectiveness not only as a communicator, but also pretty soon people are just going to think, *Oh yeah, there he is having another cow.* We may think we're being effective, but we are not. It is a self-delusion. The critic increases his or her intensity, and pretty soon, people only see a glassy-eyed and frothing-at-the-mouth critic—someone they want to avoid.

There are mothers who find themselves in this predicament who wonder why their children don't respond to them. These mothers have conditioned their children not to respond to them until they lose it. It happens like this. Mom comes in and says, "Now, kids, tonight I want you to get ready go to bed—brush your teeth, get into your pajamas, and I'll come, and we'll say prayers. First, I need you to pick up your toys and put these things away. Now, I don't want to yell or scream; I just want you to go ahead and do it. You have five minutes."

Mom leaves, and the kids think they've got time. *Mom isn't really serious yet so we can play some more.*

Mom comes back ten minutes later. "Kids, now I told you . . ."

But the children know they still have time. They've got three or four more trips until Mom finally loses it and comes back into the room furious and yelling.

Now, think the kids, *it's time to spring into action.* They respond only when Mom has lost it because that's the sign that she means it.

The point is that we don't want to be constantly critical because we will lose our effectiveness. We have to measure what we're going to say. We have to learn to pick our battles. And we have to give each other the benefit of the doubt. People change. My oldest son asked me why I wasn't as strict with our youngest child as I was with him. I said, "Because, one, I'm smarter, and two, I'm tired. I know more now, and I know when to pick my battles. With you being my oldest, I didn't know these things; everything was a battle."

We find ourselves getting wiser and a little more experienced, and we learn to pick our battles. If something is not part of our stewardship, we're better off leaving it alone. My wife's Church calling is not my stewardship. My home teaching is not her stewardship. Some people think that nagging is how to be a helpmate. There are lots of things we *could* say, but are they necessary? If the answer to these two questions, "Is it necessary?" and "Is it a part of my stewardship?" is no, then we need to back off and bite our tongues. If both of the answers are in the affirmative, then we may move to the next point on the criticism checklist.

Ask for and Receive Permission to Criticize

It's not enough just to ask for permission to share our appropriate criticism; we also must receive permission. We were at a temple sealing not long ago where Elder Ballard made a very specific suggestion to the couple. He said, "If you have something critical to say, I want you to say to your spouse, 'Sweetheart, I have a suggestion.' And then you wait for a response. And if your spouse doesn't give you permission, you don't say anything."

This principle of asking for permission to criticize is actually found in Doctrine and Covenants 26:2, which states that all things should be done by common consent. If one criticizes without asking for *and* receiving permission, he is not treating the other person as a coequal, nor as an adult, nor with respect. If one criticizes without permission, he assumes a parental role over the other person. No one has a right, even if he or she has authority, to treat another with disrespect.

If one does not receive permission to criticize verbally, he may ask for permission to communicate his criticisms in writing. The one being criticized could then read the criticisms and respond within a given amount of time, perhaps twelve hours. This option gives the frustrated critic a place to take his criticism. Writing down criticism removes much of the intimidation factor and allows the one being criticized to focus on the content of the criticism. Otherwise, the packaging of the criticism and the delivery system supersede the message. Remember, people interpret meaning by looking at facial expressions and interpreting body language. Tone of voice also distracts from the content of the message. Writing down the criticism provides focus for the critic and greater emotional safety for the one being criticized. It requires skill to keep the focus on the message and not on the messenger.

Be Alone with the One Being Criticized at a Mutually Agreeable Time and Place

In Doctrine and Covenants 42:88–89, we read that if we have a concern with someone we need to go to the person alone. If we criticize someone in front of others, his or her focus won't be on the message; it will be on a feeling of being belittled or humiliated. If that is our objective, to humiliate, then we are not really trying to communicate any honest and legitimate concern we might have. We are coupling our message with an ineffective approach.

For those who want to enjoy a close relationship, being emotionally safe is enormously important. In addition to respect and restraint, the critic who refuses to criticize in front of others is displaying loyalty to the relationship. It is hypocrisy to expect loyalty from others when loyalty is not given. A common complaint expressed by men and women is that they resent being criticized in front of their coworkers, friends, or children. The focus is not on the message but on the messenger's insensitivity. The critic becomes emotionally unsafe and is seen as disloyal. Criticism in front of others is an emotionally unfaithful act. It is astounding to those being criticized that the critic could do so with such impunity.

There are consequences for humiliating someone in front of others. Emotional closeness will suffer. Respect will be replaced by resentment. Most critics are either unaware of these consequences or it simply doesn't matter to them. It is as though the critic feels justified for giving criticism in public, and so he feels he has done nothing to deserve alienation. He expects that being "right" gives him permission. The critic assumes there will be no consequences for his self-justified behavior. His criticism is a just compensation for the behavior of the one who is being chastised.

Behavior which says, "I am free to criticize anytime, anywhere, and in front of anyone I choose," is naïve and carries tragic consequences. Ironically, even when the critic is right, he is wrong in sharing the criticism publicly. To criticize in front of others and hope that social pressure will be on the side of the critic is foolish. *The sympathy goes to the one being criticized.*

Imagine in a classroom setting, a misbehaving boy who is truly guilty of rude and insensitive conduct. The teacher calls him by name and chastens him in front of the other students. In spite of the fact that the student is wrong and the teacher is right, the students will sympathize with the one being embarrassed in front of others. In this case the teacher is right in principle but wrong in delivery.

Be in Emotional Control and Logically Explain Your Concerns

Adding emotionalism to criticism only confuses the matter. The focus should be the issue or behavior in question. It is best not to become angry, swear, or cry. Some feel this display of emotion adds emphasis to their point of view. The critic only succeeds in making himself the focus. Those who use physical or emotional intimidation as a part of their presentation once again dilute the message and divert the focus to the messenger.

It is a dysfunctional and a self-defeating behavior to criticize anyone in the heat of emotionalism. If it is too sensitive an issue and tears cannot be restrained, it would be better to write it down. Men feel manipulated when women cry. They resent it. They feel diverted from the true issue. Many women have this same response when men yell at them. Both yelling and crying shift the focus to the messenger and away from the issue or the message. We must decide whether we really want behavioral change or if we merely want to vent. If we truly want change, we must be in emotional control.

There is no such thing as righteous anger. Matthew 5:22 states, "Whosoever is angry with his brother without a cause shall be in danger of the judgment." In the Book of Mormon and the Joseph Smith translation, however, the Prophet removed the phrase "without a cause," because that was added to Matthew's writings by a biblical scribe who must have thought, *We can't really expect people to do this.* Then we have the statement in Ephesians 4:26, which was also changed by the Prophet Joseph to "Can ye be angry, and not sin?" Joseph changed it to read that we cannot be angry and not sin (see JST Eph. 4:26). People often try to justify their anger by citing the instance in the New Testament where the Savior drove the moneychangers out of the temple. According to the Greek and Hebrew origins of the words *anger* and *wrath,* these words refer to the disappointment of God. When it says that the God of heaven was angry, it doesn't mean He was up there smashing a few angels' faces in or kicking some celestial chairs over because He was really ticked off. No, the anger of God is the disappointment of God, and it comes from the Hebrew word meaning, "to expel the breath."

The only time it actually says that Jesus was angry is in Mark 3:5, where He heals a man on the Sabbath day and asks the Pharisees and Sadducees whether it is righteous to heal and to do good on the Sabbath or whether is it considered evil to do good on the Sabbath. The hypocritical leaders hold their peace in response to His question, but they want something with which to accuse Him. And it says in verse five that he "looked round about on them with anger." If we read on, we realize that His anger here is different from the kind where we're stomping mad and out of control: "He was grieved for the hardness of their hearts." Another interpretation for the word *anger,* both in the Hebrew and in Greek, is "being grieved." By the way, as He looked around at them, being grieved at the hardness of their hearts, He told the afflicted man to stretch forth his hand and healed him. So if we want to be "angry" like Jesus was angry, we have to focus on healing others, not hurting them.

What about throwing over the money tables in the temple in John 2:14–16? We assume He is angry here. However, if we read that account carefully, it becomes clear that He uses the leather thong to drive out the oxen and larger cattle. It never says He was hitting people. He did tip over the moneychanger's tables because they had made the house of prayer a den of thieves. Gentiles couldn't go into the temple, but if a gentile wanted to pray, he could go into the court of the gentiles. But these money changers had taken over the court of the gentiles so that the gentiles didn't have a place to pray, so Jesus drove them out.

We must be very careful in trying to justify our anger because "we cannot be angry and not sin." There is no such thing as righteous anger. From a psychological point of view, when we have an expectation that's not met, our first reaction is to be frustrated—not angry, but frustrated. Now, it doesn't take some of us very long to go from frustration to anger, and we assume that a particular behavior has made us angry. But anger is a choice. Remember, anger is something we learn as children. We can choose not to be angry. We can choose to smile or sing, "Have I done any good in the world today?" We can always choose something else, because there are a myriad of options from which to choose.

Many of us give ourselves permission to be mean and to say hurtful things when we are frustrated or angry, even if we have to apologize later. In the heat of anger we say anything we want to say. And when we're done saying everything we want to say, well, we may not have meant it all, but . . . We then spend an incredible amount of time trying to undo the damage that's been done. Again, there is no justification for anger. That means no yelling, no crying, no swearing, no physical or emotional intimidation or abuse in any way, shape, or form.

One man followed his wife around with a tape recorder. He recorded five hours' worth of his wife screaming at the children and at him. The judge listened to twenty minutes and granted him a divorce, the children, and the house. The judge told the woman, "I think you could best serve this family by going out and providing for it." She stood to lose five children, her husband, and her house all at once because the judge declared her an unfit mother.

It turns out that I was the one assigned by the court to deal with this situation. The woman, whom we'll call Trina, was looking at her divorce becoming final in ninety days. She came to me with her husband, who'd actually been a student of mine, and we began to talk about conflict resolution. As we sat down to have this discussion, I said to her, "Now, Trina, you seem very tense right now."

Her fists were balled and her breathing was rapid. And she said, "You would be tense, too, if you had just lost your house, your five children, and your husband."

I looked at Trina's husband and asked him if there was anything we could do. And he replied that he had told his wife, "If you will go see Dr. Lund, then maybe there's a chance."

So, under these conditions, she showed up. I said to Trina, "That puts a lot of pressure on you, doesn't it?"

"It puts a lot of pressure on you, too," she said.

I said, "Yes, it really does. So, let's start right here. You are done criticizing. You are done." I looked at her husband and said, "So, Dad, I want you to take the responsibility right now, that if a child needs to be criticized or reproved, you are going to do it." Then I looked back at Trina. "And guess what Trina. We are going to release you from being a critic. That means you are done. When you go home today (they were still in the same house), you are not just going to get the twenty-four-hour challenge, you are going to get the week—not one more word of criticism out of your mouth. You are done criticizing. It's over, and if you won't agree to this, I won't talk to you."

I asked her if she understood what criticizing was. I gave her a definition so that she clearly understood what it was, and then I said, "Now, as you leave this room today, I want you to think of yourself as a very loving person who is going to go home, and I want you to find positive things about your children. We are releasing you from criticizing because the court of the land is going to release you from your role as a mother in ninety days if this does not work. I want you to focus the time you have left to just love your children and your husband. You be the most positive person you can be. If you don't make it Trina, we are done. Because this relationship will not survive if you don't conquer your inability to manage criticism."

They had come to me on a Saturday, and she came back the next Saturday, along with her husband. When she came through the door, she erupted in tears, and I was fearful that she hadn't made it. I thought, *I'm afraid it's going to be a short meeting today.* I looked at her husband and said to him, because she was crying, "Did she not make it?"

He said, "She made it. We had the best week of our entire marriage. This was the greatest week. I can live with this woman if she's like this. I don't know why she's crying." We're not just talking about crying. Trina was sobbing, a deep, soulful sobbing.

I asked Trina to tell me what was wrong. She said, "You don't understand. Nobody understands."

And I said, "You are right, Trina, I don't understand. You should be congratulated. You made it."

Then Trina came back with, "No, you don't understand. I don't know how to love. I don't know how to love! I thought that I was supposed to be critical, and correct everything, and force the children to do their jobs by yelling because that was the way my mother was with me. I thought that was loving. I thought that was my job description—to help people change. When you released me from that responsibility and I got home, I didn't have anything to say to anybody, because when I couldn't be critical, I couldn't think of anything to say."

I was astounded. I asked her, "Didn't you do something positive with the children?"

She replied, "I didn't know what to do."

"I'm talking about sitting down and reading a book. I'm talking about going on a walk. I'm talking about singing and playing Eentsy-Weentsy Spider or whatever it takes."

"I didn't think of those things. I didn't know what to do. I didn't criticize, but I didn't know what to do. I don't know how to love."

So we had a challenge. The challenge was to teach Trina how to love. I talked to Trina about age-appropriate activities with each of her five children. "With this one, Trina, sit down and read a book. With your teenager, talk and share time and go with the girls to buy fingernail polish. Go to a ball game with the older boys; take the younger ones to the park to fly kites." In a very short period of time, Dad was the total disciplinarian, and Trina was a lover of her children.

Then I was transferred. I tried to stay in contact by phone, but I wasn't able to see Trina in person. About three years later, I saw her sitting in a meeting in which I was the speaker. She was sitting on the front row with her husband and children. I acknowledged her, and she came up and said, "Do you remember me?"

I said, "Oh, yes, I remember you, Trina. How are things going? I feel bad we didn't get through the last half of that exercise where we were talking about *appropriate* ways to share criticism."

She became very serious and said, "Things are working just fine, thank you. I focus mainly on loving the children, and if I have something critical I feel I need to say, I share that with my husband, and he has agreed to share it with the children because I'm never going back there again. Not ever!" She was afraid of falling back into her addictive pattern of being critical, and she felt like she'd been born again, born to a new kind of life, because she had eliminated criticism from her life.

Stay Focused on the Issue or Behavior in Question

We need to stay focused on the issue or the behavior and not attack self-worth. Some of us, when we get frustrated, start attacking the person. "You're so stupid," "You're so dumb," "How can anybody . . . ?" The moment we go there, we take the focus off the message and engage in a personal attack on the individual.

One's immediate family should be the greatest contributor to self-esteem and self-perception. A child who is raised with a constant bombardment of "You are worthless," "You are no good to anybody," "You are dumb, stupid, and lazy" is going to have a problem with low self-worth. In striving to be a disciple of Christ in the art of giving appropriate criticism, we are never justified in belittling the worth of another. *Never!* It cannot be tolerated. One never has the right to attack the inherent value or self-worth of another, not in jest, not in the heat of anger, not out of frustration, not out of one's own weakness. *Never! Never! Never!* This means no name-calling, no swearing, no epithets. It means no spiritual, physical, or emotional abuse. This is nonnegotiable. When someone is called "dumb" or "stupid," it is an attack on their worth. And to attack self-worth is presuming a right that the critic does not have.

Affirm Worth

Affirming worth is another way of saying that after one has reproved or criticized he needs to show "forth afterwards an increase of love toward him whom thou hast reproved, lest he esteem thee to be his enemy" (D&C 121:43).

How does one follow up a message of rejection with a message of love? It is made more difficult by the fact that the one criticized may feel rejected, withdrawn, and alienated by the giver of criticism. Human nature being what it is, inappropriately given criticism will add to the difficulty of showing forth an increase of love. The critic will often find that before he can show forth love, he has to apologize for the inappropriate way the criticism was given. He is not apologizing for the content but the delivery. If the critic allowed himself to be angry or to lose emotional control by yelling or by attacking the worth of the one being criticized, he has a self-imposed higher mountain to climb. First, he must undo the damage done by improper criticism. *It may take an hour or so for the one criticized to be receptive.* The very pattern of improper criticism destroys the credibility of the critic. Words of love mean little when loving behaviors are absent. To the one criticized, words of love seem hollow and empty, even hypocritical.

The greatest thing the critic can do to convince the one reproved of his or worth is not to repeat improperly given criticism. The critic needs to show respect by restraint. If necessary, write the criticisms down on paper. Keep the verbal airways clear of criticism. Use the verbal channels for normal and positive communication. This extra effort may be required if the critic has a problem maintaining a civil tongue. Breaking the nonproductive behavioral pattern of negative emotionalism and criticism is hard. Nevertheless, there is power in the principles of the gospel to change the most ingrained habits.

Even when criticism is appropriately given, the scriptures admonish us to show forth an increase of love. Wisdom indicates that we wait at least twenty minutes after we have criticized someone before we show forth "an increase of love." It takes that long for the adrenalin to assimilate in the body. Most of us, after having been criticized, want to withdraw and isolate ourselves. An increase of love might be a small gift of a flower, a candy bar, or a note saying, "Here are ten reasons I love you."

Once we have asked ourselves whether we have stewardship and whether our criticism is necessary, and after we learn to abstain from unnecessary criticism, we must affirm the worth of those we criticize. The more we put our lives in harmony with the teachings of the scriptures, the more the Spirit will be able to be with us. We will have less contention in our homes. We will have a greater spirit of love if we can learn to manage the negative.

Dr. John L. Lund's
QUICK-CHECK GUIDE TO GIVING APPROPRIATE CRITICISM

STEP ONE
Before You Speak, Ask Yourself Two Questions:

1. Is the criticism a part of my stewardship or business?
2. Is the criticism not only true, but is it also necessary?

If the answer to *either* of the foregoing questions is no, then back off! If the answer to *both* of the questions is yes, proceed with the following:

STEP TWO
- Ask for and receive permission to criticize.
- Be alone with the one being criticized at a mutually agreeable time and place.
- Be in emotional control and logically explain your concerns. No yelling, crying, swearing, threats, or physical or emotional intimidation.
- Stay focused on the issue or behavior in question. Do not attack self-worth! Separate the issue from ego. Protect self-worth.

STEP THREE
Affirm the worth of the one being criticized to you!

CHAPTER TWELVE

The Art of Receiving Criticism

Now that we understand a bit about the art of giving criticism, we need to talk about the art of receiving it. This is the ability, as a receiver, to take our ego, set it aside, and actually focus on the message. What if what was said to us is something that, even though it wasn't packaged in the right way, was something that would make us a better son or daughter, a better husband or wife, a better individual, or maybe make our family better? Do we have the ability to grow? We may have the ability, but are we willing? Or do we tend to take a defensive stance? Rather than become defensive, we can find creative ways to receive criticism.

It has been said that no one can hit you over the head with an emotional club that you don't first put into their hand. Being able to protect yourself from the negative effects of criticism is a part of the art and skill needed for receiving criticism. There is a desire you must possess: the desire to become your highest and best self. Without that desire, you will never be able to truly learn the art of receiving criticism. What if the criticism is valid? If you are not committed to becoming your highest and best self, you will not even evaluate the criticism on its merits. Instead, you will be distracted by the way it is said. Your desire to defend your self-esteem, your worth, or your ego will prevail.

If you are going to be successful in receiving criticism from others, it will require that you live a higher law. The single greatest challenge to receiving criticism is the ego. The higher law you will be asked to live demands that you place your ego in a safe place. Protect yourself. Otherwise, every conversation with anyone about anything becomes an issue for ego validation, where you feel that others must agree with you, that you must be right, or you have no value. This means you become so emotionally involved in defending your ideas, behavior, and ego, that you cannot receive valid criticism. You wind up defending your sense of worth, and you are not open to hear what the real issues are. Taking your ego out of the picture is a necessary step.

Going on a "Mind Walk"

Let me tell you what I do. I have a very special box. When anyone criticizes me, I immediately take my ego, my sense of worth, and put it mentally in the box. It takes me a half second. Then I go in my mind to the temple and place the box on the altar for Jesus to take care of it until I return. It works for me. However, each person has to find a way that works for him or her.

A "mind walk" is a mental journey you take the moment someone begins to offer uninvited criticism. Imagine in your mind an alarm going off, just like those noisy irritating car alarms that go off when someone touches the car. Or think of your ego being in a bank vault, and when the alarm sounds, all the doors automatically close. Huge, impenetrable, solid-steel doors, two feet thick, close off every window, door, or exit. Like the precious Mona Lisa, a priceless art treasure, your ego is protected. It is safe. Now you can venture outside the bank, because your ego is safe within the vault.

One man said his "mind walk" included a visual image of the critical person asking for the combination to the safe, and he would say, "I'm sorry, it's not available to you." He saw himself putting a package containing his ego into the safe and closing the door and spinning the dial. One very inventive woman said she had a secret Personal Identification Number (PIN) like one finds at all automatic bank-teller machines, which represented her ego and which she didn't let anyone who was toxic know, or if someone became ego-toxic, she changed her secret number.

This doesn't work for everyone, but living a higher law requires that you develop a system to protect your ego. There are unproductive and relationship-defeating behaviors such as becoming confrontational, abusive, and more toxic than the giver of criticism. Becoming totally passive and allowing ourselves to be verbally abused is equally unacceptable. The fight or flight alternatives are not as productive as a "mind walk." Some simply choose to ignore any unauthorized criticism. In other words, they don't sign for the critic's "registered mail."

I suggested to several people that they reward themselves twenty-five cents each time they were criticized. One man bought himself a new fly rod. At twenty-five cents a criticism, one young married wife bought a new pair of shoes in only a month.

Let's assume that you develop an effective "mind walk" that works for you. Your ego is safe. This means that you have removed self-esteem as an issue, thereby avoiding any emotional meltdown. You are Spock on *Star Trek*. Doctor McCoy comes ranting and screaming at you because you are not responding to his emotionalism. Although he calls you names like a "pointed-eared, green-faced, half-human freak," it doesn't bother you. You look at him and say, "Very interesting, but quite illogical." Can you imagine how long a court reporter would last if he or she kept getting emotionally involved in each court case? If the court reporter cried and wept and asked the judge for a moment to compose himself or herself, that person would be fired. You are going to "fire" the person criticizing you every time their negative emotions flair up. You do so by ignoring the packaging. Disregard the "how" and examine the "what." Separating your ego from the criticisms of others takes practice and is a highly-developed mental skill. But it can and must be done.

Step One
Stop, look, and listen

Truly listening and not reacting is difficult. There is a strong urge to want to explain, justify, or defend. This is where you "zip your lips." Don't apologize. Don't make excuses. Don't speak. Just gaze into their eyes and listen!

Remember the old-style record players? Maybe you've seen one in an attic or a museum. They played records of different sizes. They would also play at different speeds, e.g., 45, 78, or 33. Records of the same speed were placed in a stack on a metal center post. An automatic arm would extend from the side once the record was in place. A needle protruding from the arm fit perfectly into the record groves. At last! Music! It was quite primitive compared to the CDs of today. However, the old record players had an unusual characteristic. No matter where the record was playing—the beginning, the middle, or the end—if you bumped the record player, the automatic arm would stop, go all the way back to the beginning, and start all over again. That is just like people who are criticizing. If they are interrupted, they go back all the way to the beginning and start over. Sometimes they increase the tone of their voice another octave because they believe you are not listening. So listen for the issue or behavior which is the object of the critic's concern, so he or she won't have to start all over again.

Next, I'm going to ask you to write down the criticisms. This may sound like a contradiction. I've already asked you to look into the eyes of the critic and to listen to what he or she is saying. Look down only to write and then look back up into the critic's eyes. Look only at the eyes and the paper. It works, and I'll explain why.

Step Two
Write criticisms where they can be evaluated

Years of experience have verified the importance of writing down criticism. The difference between those who succeed in receiving criticism and learn from it and those who fail in this task is their willingness to follow this counsel. There are two important reasons why you should write down criticisms. The first is psychological. Writing down criticism will allow it to enter your ears, flow through your brain, down your arm, and hand to the paper. Otherwise the criticism will stay in your brain. Maybe the greatest benefit is spiritual. By writing down the criticism as an issue or behavior, you are protecting your value as a child of God. You are focusing on the issues or behaviors in question. This is a legitimate process.

Step Three
Feed back the criticism without emotion
Some people feel that unless one is emotional he or she is not serious. This is a characteristic learned in the family. It's not healthy. As mentioned before, about half of all men feel manipulated when women cry. They feel it's a diversion from the facts. Almost always, when someone is crying or yelling, it is a plea for understanding and acceptance. However, it is a diversion to ego and away from the issue. Consciously or unconsciously, crying when criticized is a reaction to feeling rejected. Sometimes, unless a person is emotional, he doesn't give himself or herself permission to express feelings. There are appropriate times for tears. The art of receiving criticism is not one of them.

Continue to write down the expectations or the frustrations. Be a court reporter. Eventually, the critic will finish. After he or she is through criticizing you, feed it back to the person without emotion. Do it just as if you were reading a recipe from a cookbook. For example, "So what you are saying is that I spend too much time talking on the phone with my friends. If I spent less time on the phone, I would have more time to devote to cleaning the house and cooking." This does not mean in any way that you agree with the person or with the evaluation or criticism. It just means you heard it.

Step Four
Excuse yourself from any immediate response and set a time and place to respond
Avoid the very, very, very big temptation to verbally or emotionally respond at this time. This is not the time to cry or to become angry or to stomp out of the room and slam a door.

You could say, "I've heard you. It wasn't easy, but believe me, I have heard you. I'm not prepared to respond now. I need some time to think about these things. I want to evaluate my ability, willingness, and energy to make the changes you've suggested. I'm not capable of anything right now but an emotional reaction. Give me three days to evaluate. I propose we meet on Wednesday at 7:00 PM at the park. I will be prepared to talk to you then."

Do not allow the critic to draw you into a conflict. Excuse yourself and be civil and kind. It is very important not to try to explain or justify the issue being criticized.

Step Five
Evaluate the criticism

It's time to be honest with yourself. It's time to pan for gold. Maybe you have never given yourself permission to be honest. Is there any truth whatsoever to these criticisms? Evaluate each one. Evaluate your time. Evaluate where you might improve even if it is not all that was asked. Don't commit to do what you cannot do in the name of appeasement. It will come back to bite you later.

Step Six
Respond at the appointed time and place

Your response will fall into one of these categories:

- I will change.
- I disagree and this is why . . .
- I need more specific information before I can make an intelligent evaluation.
- I will not change because I am unwilling or unable to do so.

Go prepared. Write down in black and white what you are willing to do.

There was a woman who had four absolutely wonderful children from a previous marriage and planned on remarrying. The stepmother of the husband-to-be was a very critical person, toxically critical. She did not want them to be married and so she told this woman that if she married her stepson, she would make life miserable for her. Not only that, she said she'd never accept the woman's children, not ever.

The woman could stand the criticism for herself, and she so married the man anyway, deciding she'd just put up with the criticism. But when this mother-in-law started criticizing her children, the woman had to draw the line. Her children were coming home in tears.

So this woman came to me, and I told her to gather her family together. These were very good children, the kind every family would love to have. I said to the children, "Do you know what? You have a toxic grandma. Now, she's a wonderful person in many ways, but she is also toxic, which means that you are never going to be able to please her no matter what you do, so here's what you need to do. You still need to be good, and you still need to be civil, and you still need to be kind, independent of whatever she is going to say. I want you to go to the family reunion, and she's going to find fault, and she's going to be critical, and you are not going to be able to avoid it. But here's the thing. The one who is criticized most gets a double-decker ice-cream cone on the way home, and the others only get a single-decker. So, can you kids keep track of who is criticized the most?"

Those kids adjusted in one outing. Grandma would be critical, and they would say, "That's one for me," rather than run off and cry as they had in the past. They would simply say, "Okay, Grandma." Then they'd figure out that Grandma had targeted Aaron or Lisa most, and that person would get their double-decker ice cream. They made a game out of it and didn't internalize all that negativity. They chose to realize that this was just how Grandma was. They weren't going to change her. This wasn't about them unless there was a legitimate issue.

One lady in my class took on the challenge to not internalize criticism but to reward herself. I said to her, "Every time your critical, super-toxic husband criticizes you, I want you to look at him and imagine that your eyes are an old-time cash register. You are going to blink when he criticizes you, and that's going to ring up one dollar. So every time he criticizes you, I want you to blink and give yourself one dollar." It wasn't long before this lady left a delightful message for me. She said, "Tell Dr. Lund I just bought an eighty-dollar pair of shoes. He'll know what I mean." I sometimes challenge my students to wear a rubber band around their wrists. When any criticism comes, they snap the band and say, "I am not going to take this in. Yes, it's painful, but I'm leaving it out here; I am not going to take it inside."

In order to gain perspective, we've got to stop, look, and listen. If we will follow this simple rule when someone criticizes us, it may prove enlightening to us. We have to stop, put our ego aside for a moment, look the person in the eyes, and listen. We're talking about looking; we're not talking about glaring. When they are done, we give them *tell back*. Tell back is where we repeat back to the sender what they've said to us, where we paraphrase what we've heard. Now, as we're listening and giving tell back, it's important to remember that it doesn't necessarily mean we need to internalize that criticism or that what's being said is true. It may simply be their perception. Once we reiterate what it is they've said to us, they confirm that, yes, that is what they meant.

Give Me a Way to Approach You with Criticism

Imagine what would happen if every relationship had a procedure whereby criticism could be passed on. But let us now focus on you becoming your highest and best self. I have a criticism of something you are doing that is counterproductive to you becoming your best self. Let's assume that my criticism is valid. How would you prefer that I approach you with a legitimate criticism? I am asking for you to give me a *way* to share my critical thought with you.

Most of us are not going to want to hear criticism, ever. For most of us, criticism is a root canal without Novocain. It is painful, and our life experience with it has not been good. "No thanks, I don't want to give you a way to approach me. Now or ever." If there is no healthy way you can be approached, you will probably have people dump on you in all the negative and dysfunctional ways they have in the past, and you can avoid the responsibility to ever improve. So what are your options?

Ways of Being Approached with Criticism
Write it down in a letter. Give me twelve to twenty-four hours to think about it, and I will give you a written response. There are several advantages to the written word. It has no facial expression, no body language, and no tone of voice. It will appear in black and white where I can read it and ponder my response. Also, with a letter I don't have to break down and cry in front of you, and I don't have to get angry.

Talk to me on the phone. I feel safe at the end of a phone line or cell phone. I can listen to you and your criticism and feed it back to you. And then I can think about it and call you back. It's the phone for me.

Face-to-face—but I have several requirements. Number one, I want you to hold my hand while you criticize me. Number two, I would like to know that you have thought about this criticism. I am asking that you bring at least one reasonable solution with each criticism. Number three, I want to know that you value me. So I am asking that you tell me two positive things you like about me for every negative thing you have to say.

Send me an e-mail; be direct and precise. Cut to the chase and tell me exactly what criticism you have.

Face-to-face with the following conditions: Tell me how painful you believe this is going to be on a scale of one to ten. If it's from one to five, I'll deal with it now. If it's from six to ten, I need time to prepare myself emotionally. I'll try to give you a fixed time within the next twelve hours. I'll write it down, but I'll need twenty-four hours to think about it. I'll get back to you within twenty-four hours of our meeting with my response.

The Red Hour: The outline for direct but kind content communication criticism is given in the next chapter. This is a face-to-face meeting of fifteen minutes. It requires people cut to the chase and focus on the issue. There can be conditions such as hold my hand, give one positive for every negative, give one solution for every criticism, etc. It can be nightly, weekly, monthly, according to need.

In addition to being able to listen and give tell back, we need to give our mate a way to approach us. Bonnie appreciates it when I write it down. But I'm thinking, *That is so inefficient when I have a mouth. When I can say it, why don't you just let me say it?* Bonnie feels like I talk better than she does, that I have the ability to win an argument even when she's right. So she wants me to write it down. I can try to discount her and trivialize how she's asked me to approach her, but I'm going to make myself less of a communicator, and the chances of her hearing the content of what I have to say are going to be significantly decreased if I don't respect a boundary she's set. So I write it down, and I give it to her. She likes the fact that it doesn't have facial expression or tone of voice. That way it's easier for her to feel like she can read it, think about it, and not be under the pressure of my immediate presence. Sometimes we need a little distancing, too. That's where writing it down comes into play. If we truly can't talk without being emotional, we need to write it down and wait until we can actually communicate without totally losing it.

We need to ask others how they'd like us to approach them. Rarely do we find someone who wouldn't want to be approached at all, someone who believes they don't make any mistakes. That's just not realistic. So, I need to give Bonnie a way to approach me. I also want to know how painful she thinks it's going to be on a scale from one to ten. If Bonnie says it's a nine, I may want time to prepare myself emotionally to receive that criticism. I may not be able to take it right then. I may be doing something productive where I don't want to be interrupted.

We should make time for our spouse to share any criticism he or she may have, and we can give the person a time frame, usually, within twelve hours of the time a giver makes a request. Often, the magnitude of the criticism has a lot to do with timing. If it happens to be a two on the Richter scale, bring it on, because a two isn't that painful. I can hear it right now. I don't need to prepare myself. I can pretty well do that. However, if the giver thinks it is a nine, I'm going to need to get myself ready for that.

My experience is that having the tools to deal with criticism allows for positive change and reduces the negativity in problem solving. When someone is brave enough to give you a way to approach him or her with criticism, and you respect the boundaries he or she has established, the probability that your criticism will be heard and truly evaluated is significantly increased. Think of how criticism is usually imparted. The giver of criticism is emotionally distraught, often angry, and emotional. The criticism is exaggerated. Terms like *always* and *never* are used, and the message is lost because the messenger is so emotionally engaged. Instead of dealing with a single issue, a multitude of criticisms are hurled at the one being criticized.

Sometimes the emotional blood spilt makes it difficult for the relationship to ever be repaired, and each party maintains an emotionally safe distance when reconciliation is attempted. When apologies are in order, forgiveness is first sought for in the manner in which the criticism was shared. The delivery system became a greater issue than the original criticism. In spite of the criticism being valid, the giver of criticism has to spend an inordinate amount of time trying to repair the damage done by the emotional overkill that came with the criticism.

There are healthy and unhealthy ways to deal with criticism. The healthiest is to have each party provide a clear pattern of approach. When those boundaries are respected, the outcome may not only be a change in the negative behavior being criticized, but also an increased bond of love. This increased bond of love is achieved when the giver of criticism shows forth after the criticism an increase of love toward the one criticized, demonstrating that the worth of the soul was greater than the criticism shared.

Dr. John L. Lund's
QUICK-CHECK GUIDE TO RECEIVING CRITICISM

STEP ONE

STOP! Immediately remove your ego from the issue or behavior being criticized.

LOOK at the person.

LISTEN. Do not defend, make an excuse, or apologize. Don't speak. *Listen!*

STEP TWO

Write the criticism down where you can evaluate it.

STEP THREE

Feed it back without emotion.

STEP FOUR

Excuse yourself from immediate response and set a time and place to respond.

STEP FIVE

Evaluate the criticism.

Step Six

Respond at the appointed time and place.

The response will fall into one of these categories:

- I will change.
- I disagree and this is why . . .
- I need more specific information before I can make an intelligent evaluation.
- I will not change because I am unwilling or unable to do so.

CHAPTER THIRTEEN

The Red Hour: Containment of Critical Words

The Red Hour is an extension of the twenty-four-hour ban on criticism. It allows for four fifteen-minute sessions a week where criticisms can be given and received. The objective is to provide an outlet for criticism in a controlled environment. It is also to teach the principles of patience and long-suffering consistent with Doctrine and Covenants 121:34–46. This means husbands and wives are not to be critical of one another for twenty-three hours and forty-five minutes for four of the seven days a week. On the other three days of the week the twenty-four-hour ban on criticism for the husband and wife is in effect. Criticisms on all of the days are to be written down and only shared during the Red Hour. However, these cannot exceed the four, fifteen-minute sessions a week for a total of one hour, the Red Hour. It is called the Red Hour after an old television program where, for one hour a week, everyone was totally honest but not brutal. They spoke the truth.

Once the four sessions have been used up, the parties must wait for a new week. The week starts on Sunday and ends on Saturday. They are not cumulative, meaning use them or lose them. Each week has only four, fifteen-minute sessions. Either spouse can call for a Red Hour session. It would be possible to have sessions on Sunday, Monday, Tuesday, and Wednesday. However, any criticism after the Wednesday session would have to wait for three days. Writing the criticisms down and waiting to discuss them one or two days later has a cooling effect, and when you bring your list of criticisms to the Red Hour session, you will find that many of your criticisms will be dropped from your list and the more important ones will come to the forefront.

Red Hour Guidelines
 Equipment Needed: A kitchen timer or portable alarm clock with a bell or buzzer.

Explanation of Roles:

There is a giver of criticism called the speaker.

There is a receiver of criticism called the listener.

It is the giver of criticism's role to follow Dr. Lund's "Quick-Check Guide for the Art of Giving Criticism." You are to set the timer or alarm clock for seven and a half minutes.

1. It is the speaker's responsibility to always ask for permission of the listener to share the criticism.
2. Be alone with the one being criticized. Go to the bedroom, bathroom, car, etc.
3. Be in emotional control and logically explain the criticisms.
4. The speaker can only comment on the issue, not on the worth of the listener. Separate ego from issue.
5. After you have explained your criticism, invite the receiver of the criticism to mirror, reflect, paraphrase, or restate what the criticisms were. Warning: The listener is not to give their opinion, comment on the criticism, or attempt to justify or explain it. They are to simply to reflect the speaker's criticisms.
6. The speaker confirms that the listener has properly reflected the criticism. If not, the speaker restates the criticism in different words and once again asks for tell back.

The seven and a half minutes pass quickly, and you will probably only have enough time to mention one or two issues. You might want to pick the one from your list of criticisms that is the most important. Once the timer goes off, the session is over regardless of who is speaking.

7. The listener or receiver of criticism is to follow Dr. Lund's Quick Check Guide for the Art of Receiving Criticism.
8. The receiver of criticism is to stop, look, and listen to the speaker.
9. The listener is to write down the criticism as the speaker gives it.
10. When called upon by the speaker, the listener feeds back the essence of the criticism he or she received without comment.
11. Now it is the other person's turn. Roles are reversed, the timer is set, and the process is repeated.

There are going to be criticisms, and many of them will be legitimate concerns. The Red Hour is an opportunity to process "whatever is bothering us." Bonnie and I have been using the Red Hour for years now, but when we first started we would use all four sessions per week. As we became more and more proficient, we would go weeks before we realized we needed a Red Hour session. Sometimes I could see Bonnie writing things down, and she would announce that we needed a Red Hour. At first it was hard to beat the habit of giving criticism at the moment of frustration. We created a job jar, where each of us would place a folded piece of paper listing odd jobs that needed to be done, jobs that could be accomplished in fifteen minutes or less. There were also personal things like a back rub or foot massage, or "put all the tools on the workbench in their proper place," or "clean out the junk drawer," etc. When someone expressed an unauthorized criticism, he or she had to take a job from the jar to pay for the violation. One time I was very frustrated because Bonnie had taken one of my books and left it in the car with the window rolled down, and the book got rained on. I walked over to the job jar, took out a paper, and then criticized Bonnie over the wet book. By the way, the job was to clean the upstairs bathroom toilet bowl.

I have a humorous memory of one of our early Red Hour sessions. Bonnie was the giver of criticism, and I was the receiver. We set the alarm clock for seven and a half minutes. Bonnie began to explain why she felt the way she did. The timer was ticking away, and before she had even gotten to her first point, the alarm went off and her portion of the Red Hour was over. She had been talking about her feelings and laying the foundation, and ding! Her time was up. This meant that she would have to wait for twenty-three hours and forty-five minutes to finish her critical thoughts. It was then my turn, but as it happened I had nothing to discuss. So Bonnie asked me, "Can I have your seven and a half minutes?"

"No way. Sometimes life is a bummer. See you tomorrow night."

Nowadays, Bonnie gets right to the point. By the time we get to the Red Hour, she has crossed many items off her list that seemed important at the time of frustration but turned out to be inconsequential. In the seven and a half minutes, she focuses on the real issues. If you are efficient, you can say a lot seven and a half minutes. The key is to cut to the chase in a Red Hour. It takes practice and skill, but it can be learned and taught.

We can even practice the principles of giving and receiving criticism in an office setting. We tried it with one particular company, where each morning we divided the employees into pairs. We wanted each of them to have a turn at being a giver of criticism and a receiver of criticism. We asked them to talk about some of the frustrations that commonly happened at this workplace, such as people not showing up at the right job site or off-colored stories being told.

So every Monday morning the employees were invited to list their recommendations. But the employers weren't going to let it turn into a complaining session; they were looking for solutions. Now, if they could resolve an issue *at the time* because it was a legitimate concern, they did. But if not, it was passed on to the supervisor for review. The sessions were ten minutes long, and there were only three rules. First, you had to follow the rules for giving and receiving criticism. Second, you had to bring at least one solution for every problem. Third, no complaining was allowed. This was a solution-oriented activity, not a gripe session.

In teaching their children to use the Red Hour, one parent reported that ten-year-old Billy claimed that the problem was his twelve-year-old brother, Brad. According to Billy, Brad's problem was that he was stupid. Billy's solution was for Brad to "wise up." This is humorous, but it points out the inability of young people—and of most people who have not learned—to "frame the issue," or clearly define the problem to resolve the conflict. With practice, it is amazing how quickly and calmly issues can be resolved. It takes time to train people in the process but in the long run, you are giving them skills that will require less of your time, not more. Rather than giving them a fish, you are teaching them *how* to fish. However, the most important people to train in the Red Hour are the married couples. By example, parents demonstrate that problems can be solved in healthy ways. Anyone can yell and scream, slam doors, run away, give the silent treatment, or any of a dozen dysfunctional and unhealthy reactions. But what a wonderful gift to give each child: parents who resolve their differences in healthy ways.

CHAPTER FOURTEEN

BINGO

When it comes to conflict resolution, BINGO becomes an acronym—a way to remember these skills of negotiation. It's part of the art of being able to resolve a conflict in healthy ways.

> B stands for "Be in emotional control."
> I stands for "Identify one issue."
> N stands for "Negotiate."
> G stands for "Generate a solution."
> O stands for "Obligate yourself with a good attitude."

B—*Be in emotional control*

1. Being in emotional control means no yelling, crying, swearing, or physical or emotional intimidation. It means you are prepared or will get yourself prepared to logically choose and discuss a conflicting point of view. Don't try to resolve a conflict when you or the other person are angry or upset. Why? Because anger will escalate negatively into attack and counter-attack until both parties are defensive. Few people ever grew up resolving problems in healthy ways. Most people were conditioned to only express their heartfelt issues while in a state of anger or emotional upset. This is why we have to develop replacement skills and replacement behaviors. This is what we are learning now—how to talk calmly about our differences of opinion.

2. Plan B. Because I have been doing this for forty years, I know there are couples who cannot begin by calmly expressing their differences. They are so conditioned to be upset that the BINGO process fails at "be in emotional control." For these couples, whether it is one or both parties, I have them write down, in black and white, their

opinion on an agreed-upon issue and go through the exact same process. This means they don't try to do it verbally; rather they do everything in writing just as if they were mutes and couldn't speak.

3. Plan C is where the couple goes through the same process, only they use their phones, and they are in different rooms. Some people are so intimidated by the physical presence of the other that they cannot focus on the issues. Plan C allows them to practice these skills verbally but in an emotionally safe physical environment.

Some do's and don'ts about being in emotional control:
- Choose a mutually agreeable time and place. You may have to leave the house, hire a babysitter, or meet in the garage in the car.
- Be alone with the person. The sheer presence of others will shift the focus from the issue to self-awareness. People become defensive when other people are around. (The exception is an agreed-upon coach or third party.)
- Stay focused on the issue or the behavior. Do not attack self-worth. Separate the issue from the other person's worth.
- Affirm the other person's worth to you. Often, your concerns involve a criticism of the other person's behavior. This means you are asking for behavioral change. Even if you follow the above guidelines, you may still encounter a degree of defensiveness.
- Since defensiveness is a defense of one's self-worth, why not address the issue of his or her worth directly? Staying in emotional control and affirming his or her worth to you will help you focus on your original concern and not get sidetracked into a brawl of accusatory words about your worth or the other person's.

I—*Identify one issue.*

We are not going to talk about our entire lives and resolve all of the world's problems, including world peace, in our negotiating session. We are going to start with one issue, an issue we agree upon, and we will stick to that issue. Or each party can identify one issue he or she would like to address and then flip a coin to see which issue will be dealt with in this session.

Identifying one issue and succeeding in an exchange of understanding requires the speaker or message-sender to be a content communicator and the listener to be an active listener and to give tell back. For the speaker to be a content communicator, he or she is required to say what he or she means and mean what he or she is saying. It cannot be cruel, brutal, or delivered in an unkind manner. It can be honest and direct and focused on the issue. The message-sender cannot expect the listener to read minds, facial expressions, or intonations of voice. There can be no hint dropping, sarcasm, or indirect forms of communication.

Tell back is repeating back the information you received. Tell back is not feedback. Feedback involves giving your opinion. Tell back is also known as *repeat back* or *reflective listening*. It is simply repeating back what you heard or paraphrasing it. Examples of tell back are, "So what I heard you say is . . ." or "Your issues seem to be . . ."

Some people find it helpful to take notes. Because it is often hard for the listener to be quiet and not interrupt the speaker, it is also beneficial to use author and motivational speaker Steven Covey's idea of a "talking stick." A talking stick is a pen or a pencil the speaker holds while he or she is speaking. A person can only talk, comment or speak when it is his or her turn to hold the talking stick.

Remember, we may never agree on some issues. Some issues may have to be postponed. Work on the areas you are both willing to explore. Only resolve one issue at a time.

Let's see how this would work:

1. Person A is to talk for two minutes on his or her chosen topic (for practice, about grounding teenagers for breaking family rules). Set a timer or look at a watch. Go! Remember, person A is to use a pen or pencil as a talking stick.
2. At the conclusion of two minutes, person A, the speaker, gives the talking stick to person B. The listener is to give tell back to the speaker. Remember, tell back is paraphrasing the information you received. "So what I heard you say is this . . ."
3. Person B, the listener, gives the talking stick back to person A, the original speaker. Person A is to *confirm* that he or she has been understood. "Yes, that is what I said." If the speaker does not feel understood, then he or she needs to clarify his or her position. A successful exchange of understanding does not mean agreement. It means you have communicated your opinion.
4. Now reverse roles. Person B has the talking stick and two minutes to communicate his or her issue about grounding teenagers for breaking family rules. Person A is now the listener.
5. After two minutes of listening, the listener gives only tell back by reflecting the concerns of person B.
6. This time, person B confirms he or she had been understood.

The following story illustrates how important it is that we develop the skills of listening and providing tell back. Our son is a navigator on a nuclear submarine, the USS *Helena*. I had the privilege of going on an overnight cruise with him. These subs are huge, and my stepfather, who was a WWII submarine commander, came along as well. When I asked my stepfather what he thought about the *Helena,* he said you could put four of the submarines he had served on in just this one.

While at sea, the order was given by the commanding officer to submerge the ship. There is quite the chain of command.

The officer of the deck repeated back not only the order but identified himself as the one receiving the command: "Submerge the ship, Officer of the Deck, aye."

The officer of the deck next spoke to the diving officer who's called "the dive": "Dive, submerge the ship, make your depth one five zero feet."

The dive repeated back, "Submerge the ship; make your depth one five zero feet, Dive, aye."

The dive then said to the chief of the watch, "Chief of the Watch, on the IMC (ship's microphone) dive, dive two blasts of the diving alarm, dive, dive."

The chief of the watch repeated, "On the IMC, dive, dive, two blasts of the diving alarm, dive, dive, Chief of the Watch, aye."

The officer of the deck, looking through the periscope, called out, "Decks awash."

The dive then said to the plainsman, called "the plains": "Plainsman, full dive on the fairwater planes."

The plainsman then repeated back, "Full dive on the fairwater planes, Dive, Plains, aye."

The dive then addressed the helmsman, called "the helm," who controlled the angle of the ship's dive, "Helm, five-degree down bubble."

The helmsman said, "Five-degree down bubble, Dive, Helm, aye."

I later asked my son, "Are they a little slow on this ship? Everything gets repeated so many times."

My son put his hand on my shoulder and said, "Dad, how many mistakes would you like us to make aboard a nuclear submarine?" There was no room for error.

There is more fire power on board a modern-day ballistic-missile submarine than on all of the submarines in WWI and WWII combined. The only thing I could think to say when I thought about the massive power and potential for destruction was, "Make your depth one five zero feet. Five-degree down bubble, Navigator, Father, aye." Later, I learned that the navy refers to this as *repeat back.*

N—*Negotiate*

What is negotiation? Negotiation begins when both parties in the marriage acknowledge that marriage is a relationship of equals. As equals, you will have different points of view! Negotiation begins when you are open to alternatives in addition to your own opinions. Conflict negotiation is sometimes conflict management, which means you agree to disagree without being disagreeable.

The difference between a *negotiation* and an *argument* is the *willingness* to respect a different point of view and allow for fairness in coming to a mutually acceptable agreement. The first key to negotiation is fairness and a willingness to give and take. The second key to successful negotiation is that both parties walk away from the agreement with something important to each of them. The third key is a willingness to support the decision with a good attitude.

Negotiation is about looking for mutually acceptable alternatives. Brainstorming is a way to explore mutually acceptable alternatives. The rules for brainstorming are simple. Think and write down as many alternatives as you can. No negativism. During the brainstorming session, do not reject any ideas or make any negative comments. This is the time to explore options.

Not all decisions can be made in a single session. Indeed, it would not be wise to force a decision because of time constraints. After a good brainstorming session, take a break. Sleep on it and set a time to get back together unless you both feel good about an obvious option.

When you can't agree, you have options:

- Choose an option you can both support.
- Defer to the one to whom it matters most.
- Take turns (meaning this time you will do it one way and another time you will do it another way).
- Remember, you are never expected to agree to anything illegal, immoral, or against your basic core values.

Now, if we aren't in emotional control, we are not prepared to negotiate. Let's say that Bonnie and I have a difference of opinion. How are we going to resolve that difference? First of all, we need to hear her opinion, and then we need to hear mine. And can we agree to disagree without becoming disagreeable? Remember, marriage is a relationship of equals. This means we have to be willing to compromise and negotiate all things except those that are illegal or immoral.

In order to be able to negotiate effectively, we have to develop the skill of listening attentively, listening without interrupting. Remember the concept of the talking stick? The rule is that you can't talk unless you have the stick.

What I have found with a number of us, myself included, is that we need to have something to help us learn this skill.

For instance, Bonnie and I are talking. I take the stick and say, "I think we should go to Puerto Rico on our next vacation because I would really like to go there. I speak Spanish, and it's been a long time and I really want to do it. So that would be really important to me. That is where I would like to go on our vacation. So, do you think we should go to Puerto Rico? You speak Spanish, too, and you would really enjoy having a vacation there." Bonnie then takes the talking stick back, and now the most important part of this is that she confirms that, yes, she understands. It doesn't mean she agrees. It means she understands. And if Bonnie doesn't understand, she always does a great job of paraphrasing and giving me tell back, not her opinion—this is not about her opinion. This is about her ability to listen and give me tell back. So, Bonnie tells me back, and I say, "Yes, that's right."

Negotiation begins with hearing one opinion, in this case, mine, and then hearing the second opinion. "What do you think?" And Bonnie says, "I think this year that it would be better for us to go to Hawaii because our children are stationed there. And it would be a good chance to see them." And I interrupt her with, "But I don't want to go to Hawaii." See, that is inappropriate. I am interrupting her. I can't do that. She's got the stick. We don't want it to become a tomahawk. (I knew a couple who had the assignment to practice using the talking stick, and they came back with a long broom stick. They said, "We have to be this far apart when we talk.")

So Bonnie wants to go to Hawaii. And as it's now my turn with the talking stick, I say, "Bonnie, what I heard you say is that you would rather go to Hawaii because our children are currently stationed there and it would be a good opportunity to visit with them, and you're thinking that we may not get that opportunity if we don't go."

And Bonnie replies, "Yes, that's how I feel. I would like to go to Hawaii. You've got it." Now that is two opinions being shared respectfully.

Another aspect of negotiation is brainstorming. In a true brainstorming session, there is only one rule, and that is, there is no negativism. We take all ideas.

Bonnie asks, "What are some of the other ideas?"

I offer, "I want to go to Puerto Rico or Costa Rica, and you want to go to Hawaii. What else? If we can't do either of those, what else can we do?"

And Bonnie, ever the visual, comes back with, "Well, we could stay here and work on our house."

And I say, "Okay, that's one option. What do you think should go on the list?"

"Well, we could talk about our cabin in Park City."

"We could talk about that."

"We could rent a cabin for a week in Park City."

"Oh, that's a good idea."

One time my stake president said to me, "You know, we really practiced this with my family. We would do this stick thing back and forth in our home. I didn't realize how much I thought they understood when they really didn't understand." He'd learned a valuable lesson as demonstrated in the following story.

This stake president's daughter asked him if she could take the family car. "I'm just going to drive down the street a couple of blocks," she said.

Her father said, "There is no reason for you to take the car. I think you are being a bit lazy. You can walk down there. You don't need to take the car every time you want to go two blocks. Exercise is good for you."

Well, the girl started to cry. And her mother walked over to the girl, handed her the talking stick, and said to her husband, "Do you remember this?"

Now it was the daughter's turn. "Dad, I just did my hair, and it's the junior prom tonight, and I didn't want my hair all windblown. I need to borrow something from my friend. That's why I want to borrow the car."

Humbled, Dad said, "Take the car." Once he understood what the real issue was, there was no issue. She wasn't being lazy, that was only his assumption. This man told me, "You cannot believe the number of misunderstandings we've cleared up just by understanding what the other person's position was."

The truth is, that in addition to hearing what we want to hear, most of us have learned how to fight and quarrel. We've learned how to win and get our way, but we haven't learned how to negotiate. In a relationship of equals, we have to compromise and solve things at a pace we are both comfortable with. If God Himself is not above negotiation, then we ought not to be above negotiation. In the Old Testament, the Lord gives Moses a higher law for the people of Israel. But when Moses takes it to them, they can't live it. So Moses breaks the tablets, goes back to the mountain, and God gives another law, a law Israel can live (see Exodus 32–34). And how about bargaining? The Lord asked Abraham to find fifty righteous souls. If Abraham found these souls, He would spare the city (see Genesis 18). If God is not above negotiation, we ought to be able to negotiate.

Negotiation begins when we are open to an opinion other than our own because we recognize that in a relationship of equals, it requires that we move together in a spirit of unity. And in order to be unified, sometimes we are going to go one hundred and eighty degrees differently than we'd like. But we are going to do it your way this time. Next time we will do it mine. We'll simply take turns because we are on completely opposite poles on this one.

Now, we need not violate any moral code by negotiating. Most of the time, what we negotiate is not about our moral rectitude. Not everything's a ten on the Richter scale of life. We can't win everything. And we can't think that if everybody doesn't do everything we want, we will use all forms of manipulation and coercion to try and win our point. That is not negotiation.

G—*Generate a solution*

Bonnie and I discuss which of the options we can agree upon at this time. And let's say that we pick out one, and maybe it's neither one of the things we suggested; it's a third option. Or maybe because it means so much to Bonnie this time that the kids are in Hawaii, I'll say, "You know what, dear, I've been to Hawaii many, many times, but I will be happy to go back again because it would mean a lot to you. But next time, I would like to do it my way." So, even though I'm acquiescing, I'm going with a positive attitude. "We're going to go and have a great visit with the kids!"

O—*Obligate yourself to have a good attitude*

Obligating yourself is about implementing the agreed-upon solution. Once we've made a decision, we obligate ourselves to have a good attitude. We enthusiastically support the decision. I am not going to go to Hawaii to sulk at the reef or stay inside and say, "I hope you are happy. You won; we are here in Hawaii. So you go out and enjoy yourself, because I am not going out. We did it your way, you know. But, you won, so there."

Latter-day Saints understand the doctrine of the sustaining vote. It happens when anyone is called to serve in the ward, stake, or general Church offices. To sustain means you will do all in your power to see that the person or the issue is successful. Years ago, at a fireside in California, President Marion G. Romney observed that when an issue came before the Quorum of the Twelve, each member of the Quorum would express his opinion on the issue at hand, starting with the youngest member by ordination. After each opinion was expressed, a vote was taken. Let's say the vote was seven to five. Next, the president of the Quorum of the Twelve would call for a vote to sustain the decision of the majority. Obviously, the vote about opinion was over. It was no longer an issue of whose opinion would prevail. The sustaining vote was now about common consent. It was about unity and oneness. Regardless of how passionate each one may have felt about his opinion, that part was over. The new issue was unity.

Obligating yourself to support the negotiated agreement, even if it's one hundred and eighty degrees opposite of what your opinion may have been, is the current focus. It cannot be a halfhearted support. Even if you cannot agree and you wind up taking turns and it is the other person's turn, you should support that decision with a great attitude. Obligating yourself may be the most important part of the negotiation process. The time for brainstorming, exploring options, debating, and rehashing differences is over. It is now the time to sustain the agreed-upon solution. The key to the success of negotiation is our enthusiastic support at the end. We make it a good experience.

There was once a couple who had about the equivalent of twelve thousand dollars. And the man said to his wife, "Honey, this is great. We have twelve thousand dollars. Let's take it and go on a vacation. We haven't seen some of our family in years. We'll travel in the month of July and see relatives we haven't seen for a long time. It will be great! Let's just do it."

The wife said, "Oh, honey, no. I've recovered the re-coverings of the re-covered re-coverings on our couch. Can't we get some new furniture? This is a golden opportunity. For twenty years we've had this same furniture. Please, can we get some new furniture?"

So they went through their options, and they were in emotional control. They needed to decide what to do with their money. And they needed to negotiate, perhaps something like this: "Honey, let's take half the money, and we'll go on a little less of a vacation, and we will buy a little less furniture and then we both have what we want." That's probably what I would have done. That's not what this couple did.

This couple agreed that he would go ahead and take half of the money and go on a separate vacation. Now, she wanted time to go shopping. And she didn't want him along. She wanted to enjoy her shopping experience. Revel in it. Backstroke in it. She didn't want to be rushed. So he came back from his vacation, and, by the way, they had a good attitude about it. When he came home from the vacation, she didn't say, "Don't sit on my new furniture!" She was delighted to show him her new furniture. And he was delighted to sit down on that new furniture and tell her about his wonderful trip. At least that is the story that President and Sister Kimball told (see Kimball, Edward L. and Andrew E. *Spencer W. Kimball*, Salt Lake City: Bookcraft, 1977, 115).

We may not have done things that way, but let's not be too condemning. This worked for them because they decided to have a good attitude about the decision they came up with. They came to it, and they supported the decision with a good attitude, just like the Quorum of the Twelve does.

Many of my generation grew up and grew closer together hoeing beets and picking up rocks on our ward and stake welfare farms. As a deacon I was asked what we raised on our Puget Sound Stake Welfare Farm. I replied, "Rocks, I think," because that was our job as deacons—picking up rocks. (We actually raised cucumbers.) President Harold B. Lee, along with President Marion G. Romney, created the welfare program of the Church. President Benson referred to President Romney as "Mr. Welfare" (Benson, "All Is Holy Where This Man Kneels." *Ensign,* July 1988). Imagine what President Romney's feelings must have been when he was asked to sustain a decision by the Quorum of the Twelve to abandon the welfare farms he'd personally helped create and supervise for three decades!

Regardless of his personal opinion, when asked for a sustaining vote, President Romney raised his hand to the square. President Hinckley, who served with President Romney as a counselor in the First Presidency, bore testimony about all the decisions of the Quorum of the Twelve and the First Presidency: "If there is a lack of unity, there follows an absence of action" (Hinckley, "In Counselors There Is Safety," *Ensign,* November 1990, 48). President Romney knew that the spirit of unity was more important than being right in our own minds—even about a dearly-held personal opinion.

If we'll follow these guidelines of being in emotional control, identifying one issue, and negotiating—even if we have to use the talking stick and train our children to do so during family home evenings—and we then generate solutions and obligate ourselves to a good attitude, we'll find that we are able to resolve all kinds of conflicts in healthy ways. There will not only be less contention in our homes, but we will also have a greater spirit of love and unity. We will feel better about our relationships, about our families, about everything.

CHAPTER FIFTEEN

Apologizing and Forgiving

Now we are going to talk about apologies and forgiveness. There seems to be a great misunderstanding about what an apology is. We actually use terminology that itself is a misnomer because we talk about "giving an apology," when in reality, a person who *gives* an apology truly takes responsibility for any hurt, heartache, or sorrow they may have caused, either advertently or inadvertently.

Whether I bump you off of a two-story building or shove you off, the consequences are the same for you. What doesn't matter in the end is my intent. Some feel that if they caused someone hurt when they didn't mean to, they are free of any obligation. But whether an offense is accidental or intentional, we have to own it. And that is why when we have conflict with our neighbor, we must lay our gift upon the altar and reconcile things with our neighbor first. With the reconciliation process, it's more important that if I caused you any hurt, heartache, or sorrow, I acknowledge it, feel sorry for it, and apologize, even if it was done inadvertently.

An apology, then, is taking responsibility for whatever that wrong may be. What an apology isn't, is an explanation. "Well, you see, I didn't really mean to do that . . ." An apology is, "Bonnie, I would like to apologize. I am sorry."

Let's take an example of a nonapology. Let's say that I'm apologizing for something as serious as adultery. We can imagine the intense heartache associated with adultery. I might say, "I just wanted you to know that I don't know how we are going to live, but I don't expect you to find forgiveness in your heart for me. I want to tell you that I'm genuinely sorry and that I am going to ask for your forgiveness. I hope that at sometime you will be able to forgive me. I just wished that you would have been warmer at the time . . ."

I was doing okay until I tried to transfer responsibility for my behavior. The moment I began to try to explain myself, I stopped truly apologizing. I often counsel my students not to ask the *why* question because there is only one answer to the *why* question. Now, it doesn't have to be the case of adultery. It can be anything. "Why did you do that?" The answer is always, "I made a poor choice. I did it; it isn't anybody else's responsibility. It's not about what you did or didn't do. Because the truth is that it doesn't matter what you do or don't do. I make choices, and I am accountable, and I chose to do it." That is the only answer. Is there an answer that I could give that would bring you peace? There is not. The only appropriate answer is one where I accept accountability for my behavior and offer an apology that is not an explanation. Giving an apology is accepting responsibility.

Forgiveness is an interesting principle in and of itself. It's something about which God is very jealous. And that is His right. Vengeance is the Lord's. Now, the Lord is very clear about our responsibility. One of the greatest sins we could ever commit, even greater than the sin of adultery, is the sin of not forgiving. It's next in seriousness only to the unpardonable sin of a son of perdition. And the reason for that is we are telling the Lord that what He did in completing the Atonement doesn't count, that we reserve the right to choose who we are going to forgive and not forgive.

There is no question as to how clear the Lord is on this point. In Doctrine and Covenants 64:8–9, we read, "My disciples, in days of old, sought occasion against one another and forgave not one another in their hearts; and for this evil they were afflicted and sorely chastened. Wherefore, I say unto you, that ye ought to forgive one another; for he that forgiveth not his brother his trespasses standeth condemned before the Lord." And listen to this: "For there remaineth in him the greater sin." We may say, "But Lord, all I am doing is not forgiving. He or she committed adultery. And I am just not forgiving, and you're telling me that my not forgiving him or her is greater than the sin of adultery?" The answer is absolutely. This is one principle we cannot toy with. There is no leeway here on the Lord's part. He makes it unmistakably clear in verses ten and eleven: "I, the Lord, will forgive whom I will forgive, but of you it is required to forgive all men. And ye ought to say in your hearts—let God judge between me and thee."

In Mosiah 26:29, we have another strong statement. Alma is fearful that he will do wrong in the sight of the Lord, so he pleads in mighty prayer about what to do in regulating the affairs of the Church. And here's what he is told: "Therefore I say unto you, go; and whosoever transgresseth against me, him shall ye judge according to the sins which he has committed; and if he confess his sins before thee and me, and repenteth in the sincerity of his heart . . ." Now, who is going to judge if a person's been sincere?

In the Church, we have stake presidents and bishops who are given the keys of judgment. That's their specific charge. The rest of us are called to love. "And if he . . . repenteth in the sincerity of his heart, him shall ye forgive, and I will forgive him also. Yea, and as often as my people repent will I forgive them their trespasses against me. And ye shall also forgive one another your trespasses; for verily I say unto you, he that forgiveth not his neighbor's trespasses when he says that he repent, the same hath brought himself under condemnation" (Mosiah 26:29–31). We may not think our neighbor is sincere. But we are not to judge.

Now, before we go on, we need to clarify one thing. Just because the Lord expects us to forgive, it doesn't mean He expects us to trust. Trust is not about forgiveness. We are to love our fellowmen, treat them with respect, and forgive them. But trust is a function of *their* behavior. Not of ours. Trust means *they are where they say they are going to be, and they are doing what they said they were going to be doing.*

Those who have teenagers will understand this principle immediately. We can love our teenagers but not trust them. Love and trust can be separated. We can't say, "I can't forgive this person because I don't know if I can trust him. Moreover, I need a guarantee that nothing will ever go wrong in the future. That is when I will become forgiving." That's not an option because the Lord says we are required to forgive. Are you really unwilling to trade your sins? Because if we are unwilling to forgive, we are telling the Lord that what He did in Gethsemane did not count. Forgiving doesn't mean we have to be trusting of the offender and unwise about interacting with them. Forgiving means we will turn it over to the Lord for judgment.

A quick example will suffice: A woman was molested by her father, and when it was discovered, he was sent to jail, divorced, and eventually released from prison. Fifteen years went by and he remarried. The daughter that was molested came to me and said the whole family was putting pressure on her to forgive and move on. We went through the forgiveness session that will be described in chapter sixteen. I said to her, "We need to be clear about this. You can *never* trust him, even though you have forgiven him. You don't let your children stay overnight at his place, not ever. Nor are you expected by the Lord to be all huggy-kissy and pretend nothing happened just to please your family. You are not required to have any relationship with him except one of civility. If you want to go to a family reunion where he is, fine, but you don't have to be in the family photo if you don't want to. It is up to you to set the boundaries. Forgive, yes. Trust, no. After that, have whatever level of relationship you are comfortable with. Don't let your family convince you that if you have truly forgiven, you have to embrace him and trust him. You do have to forgive him and turn judgment over to the Lord. You don't have to trust him or reestablish a warm relationship."

Trading Our Sins

I can picture Bonnie showing up to the Lord someday with a little knapsack on her back with her sins in it. She's taking her sins and coming down the primrose path.

She shows up at the altar with the Lord, and the Lord says, "Well, Bonnie, good to see you. What have you got there?"

Bonnie replies, "Well, I've got my sins, Lord."

"Why don't you lay them there on the altar?"

"Do we have to forgive absolutely everyone for absolutely everything they have done to us? Lord, does that include John?" Bonnie asks.

"I thought about giving you an exception on that one, Bonnie. But no, it also includes him."

"What if I can't?"

"Then you might as well take those sins back."

"What?"

"I can't accept your sins."

"What?"

"I can't. I'd like to but I can't."

"Wow, you mean unless I am willing to forgive, you won't?"

"I can't. It's not that I'm not willing. It's that I can't."

"I see."

"Think of the Lord's Prayer, Bonnie. 'For if ye forgive men their trespasses, your heavenly Father will also forgive you: But, if ye forgive not men their trespasses, neither will your Father forgive your trespasses.' I can't. The Father hasn't given me authority to do that. So, Bonnie, do you forgive everyone, including John?"

"All right, yes. Yes, I do."

"By the way, where is John?"

"Well, Lord, he has two gunnysacks full of sins, and so he will be along any minute."

John finally arrives. He swings his two gunnysacks upon the altar and stands on his tiptoes to see over the pile. "Lord, it's me."

"Well, John, what are you here for?"

"I heard that there was a great deal going on. I get to trade in all my sins if I'm willing to forgive everyone else for theirs—whatever heartache or sorrow they have caused me. If I am willing to do that, is that true?"

"Absolutely."

"That's the best deal I have ever made. I accept!"

Isn't it interesting that Melchizedek Priesthood ordinances aren't performed for groups? All Melchizedek Priesthood ordinances are performed *individually*. When we do the work for the dead, we do it one by one. We are to consider ourselves as Adam and Eve, the only man and woman on earth. The Prophet Joseph Smith said that the past, present, and future are one eternal round with God, that God is not bound by the same time we are (see Smith, Joseph Fielding. *Teachings of the Prophet Joseph Smith,* Salt Lake City: Shadow Mountain, 1977, 220). Einstein was right. Time *is* relative. It is relative to the sphere in which we travel. A day on Kolob is equal to one thousand years on this earth (see Abraham 3:4). We read in Alma 40:8 that "time only is measured unto men." The Lord is able to step from the eternal present into our present, listen to our prayers, and return to the eternal present and not lose what we would think of as time. Though it may be difficult for our finite minds to understand, we can take comfort in Mosiah 4:9: "Believe in God; believe that man doth not comprehend all the things which the Lord can comprehend." Therefore, we can accept it on faith that God has the ability to deal with each one of us as if we were His only child. He does so personally. We need not assume that God assigns this kind of a chore to anyone else when He would chastise the brother of Jared for three hours for failing to call upon the Lord in his prayers (see Ether 2:14).

In 3 Nephi, the resurrected Christ ministers to twenty-five hundred people, who come to touch Him one by one. He picks up the little children and blesses them one by one (see 17:21, 25). The point is that *all* Melchizedek Priesthood ordinances are performed individually. The Atonement was a priesthood ordinance.

Christ was foreordained before the foundations of the world (see 1 Peter 1:20). He was ordained to the priesthood assignment of carrying out the Atonement. When He entered the Garden of Gethsemane, it was much like Moses' entering the mount of transfiguration. The same thing happened when the Savior Himself entered the mount of transfiguration and when He went into the wilderness to fast for forty days to commune with the Father. When He entered into that state, He left time as we know it. In this state, time no longer holds one prisoner. Death, as we know it, is suspended. So when the Savior entered the Garden of Gethsemane, and entered that translated state, He was able to carry out a personal Atonement for *each* person. In this priesthood ordinance, He took your name through the temple of Gethsemane, and then He came back and picked up mine.

When He says, "How exquisite you know not, yea how hard to bear" (D&C 19:15), though we can never fully comprehend the Atonement, we can have a small sense of appreciation for what occurred in that experience. A protestant minister friend of mine once asked me if I had a personal relationship with Jesus. I remember looking at him, and as tears came to my eyes, I thought about the Savior entering the temple of Gethsemane to take my name through. And in all sincerity, I said to him, "In ways that I do not have the ability to express, I believe that I have a personal relationship with Jesus. And I believe that you have a personal relationship with Jesus."

So when we think about the Atonement, let's not think about the Savior in some universal way. "I am going to suffer for all liars, and for all cheaters, and for all this and for all that." No, we need to think about Jesus taking our name specifically. Why is it that when we remember His sacrifice through the ordinance of the sacrament, we don't just have the bishop or stake president stand up and take the bread for all of us, in our behalf? We break the bread and pass it to one another, one by one, because it is symbolic of that very Atonement.

When Jesus asks us to forgive, we don't have to trust. There are some people we should not trust, even if we forgive them. The Lord does not expect us to be vulnerable or stupid. Nevertheless, we do need to be willing to forgive even though we may never forget. A lot of people assume that if they forgive somebody, they must forget. Now, the Lord says that He's not going to remember it anymore, but *we* are going to remember it. It is *how* we remember it that is the issue when we're talking about forgiving someone else. Although we don't have to remember it with joy, if we remember all the agony the sin or pain brought us, we may not truly be forgiving.

The key is to remember with a sense of, "Thank goodness for the Atonement of Jesus Christ, that in my willingness to forgive my spouse, my child, my mother, my father, my stepfather, whomever—my sins will also be forgiven me. I'm so grateful for that Atonement."

When I deal with people who have forgiveness issues, I often ask them to write a letter, and not necessarily a letter they're going to send. In some cases, the person about whom the letter is being written is deceased. I encourage them to be totally honest, to write about how that person has caused them hurt, heartache, or sorrow, and not to hold back anything. Then I have them read that letter to an empty chair, if the person is deceased and gone, or if that person is still living but there would be nothing productive about sending the letter. I try to help them understand the importance of prayerfully considering whether writing a letter would be edifying or not. Doctrine and Covenants 50:23 makes it clear: "That which does not edify is not of God." Sometimes we have to use wisdom and judgment, and we may need to counsel with priesthood leaders. Each circumstance is individual.

When the offended one has finished reading his or her letter to that empty chair, I ask him or her to say to the chair, "I forgive you, and I turn you over to God." It is vitally important that we transfer the judgment of sins to the Savior.

The following story illustrates the importance of this concept. A while back, in Southern California, a woman was stalked by an evil man who followed her to a grocery store. As she approached her car with her two little girls and a sack of groceries, unbeknownst to her, this man had parked beside her car and was waiting for her. And when she opened up the trunk to put the groceries in, he came up behind her, knocked her unconscious, threw her in the back of the car, drove her off, and subsequently violated her in a motel room.

The man thought he'd killed her with his knife as he left the scene, but she didn't die. He didn't know when he came back later and wrapped her in the bathroom shower curtain that she was still alive. He was in the process of carrying her body out of the motel room when she began to groan. He panicked. Dropping her, he grabbed his gun and put it to her temple. She moved slightly as he pulled the trigger, and the bullet took out both her eyes and the bridge of her nose. Incredibly, she survived. A man had come out of his room when he'd heard the gunshot, wrestled with the assailant, but he got away. However, the police caught him He served seven years in prison and was released.

This woman's husband could not cope with the fact that she'd been violated, so he left her. Now this woman had to overcome the adversity of learning how to deal with being blind and violated and the mother of two little girls, all on her own. I first heard her story at Mission Viejo High School, where my daughter was graduating. This woman spoke about overcoming adversity. As she began, the kids were buzzing in the bleachers. But as the story became more and more unbelievable, the kids became silent.

Her daughters, standing on either side of her, had come with her that day. They often did. After she told her story, she said, "I like to give you an opportunity to ask me questions. So, if there are any questions, there's a microphone that has been prepared, and you can line up behind that microphone and ask me any questions you would like until our time is up."

About two hundred of the three thousand students piled out of the stands and formed a line. The first question was "How much time do you spend thinking about that man and the fact that he is free? You said he's out now, and that he did seven years, and you worried about him coming after you again. Are you worried about that? How much time do you spend thinking about him, and do you think that what's happened is fair?"

Her answer astounded me. This woman said, "I get that question wherever I go. People ask me that question as if they wanted me to spend my time in regret and in complaint and mourning over that which I cannot change. Well, let me tell you young people something. I've given him all of me that he's ever going to have. And I am not going to give him my todays, and I am not going to give him my tomorrows." There was stunned silence. Then the kids stood up and started clapping. They knew that she'd said something true, and they were proud of her for having that kind of courage.

The question we must ask ourselves is what can we do with the past? Can we change it? We can go back and relive it if we want to. We can spend hours and hours reliving it. "Of all sad words of mouth or tongue, the saddest are these: It might have been!" (Whittier, John Greenleaf. *The Complete Poetical Works of Whittier.* Boston: Houghton Mifflin, 1894, 48). We can live in the land of complaint and regret, but in actuality, there are only two constructive things we can do with the past. One is to learn from it, and the other is to forgive and count our blessings. Anything else we do with our past will take us like a freeway to Depression City. It's a one-way street to misery and depression when we chose not to forgive. Is there anyone here who can go back and change the past? Even the Atonement of Jesus Christ does not go back and change the past; the Atonement compensates for the past, but it does not change it.

We have learned that frustration comes from unmet expectations. What if we refuse to let go of the expectation of wanting to change the past? What if our expectation is impossible and yet we hang onto it anyway? What if I wanted wickedness to be happiness? Eternal law is clear on this point. Wickedness may bring temporary pleasure, but it cannot bring long-term joy. The fruit, the very bitter fruit, of wickedness, is regret and misery. There is only one way to escape regret and misery, and that is by abandoning wickedness, repenting, and trusting in the love and forgiveness of our Savior. Alma instructed his son Corianton: "Wickedness never was happiness" (Alma 41:10).

Look at Lucifer, who is the embodiment of hell, and what is his hell but to want wickedness to be happiness (Helaman 13:38)? And yet Lucifer lives every day in a state of misery because what he wants is impossible. Another Book of Mormon father named Lehi said to his son, Jacob, that because Lucifer "had fallen from heaven, and had become miserable forever, he sought also the misery of all mankind" (2 Nephi 2:18). Later in the same discourse he informed his son that all of us "are free to choose liberty and eternal life, through the great Mediator of all men, or to choose captivity and death, according to the captivity and power of the devil; for he seeketh that all men might be miserable like unto himself" (2 Nephi 2:27). The

Prophet Joseph Smith taught that in hell, "a man is his own tormentor and his own condemner" (*Teaching of the Prophet Joseph Smith*, 357). Hell and the "gulf of misery" are synonyms (see Helaman 5:12; 1 Nephi 12:16). One of the greatest talks given in this dispensation was by Elder James E. Talmage. In it he announced, "To hell there is an exit" (Conference Report, April 1930, 97).

In and through the Atonement of Jesus Christ, the eternal scale of justice and mercy are balanced. The gospel, which means "good news," is that through repentance and the confession and forsaking of our sins we can escape the misery of an afflicted conscience. Once we have repented we may remember our sins. But, when we have cause to reflect upon our sins it will be with a sense of gratitude for the Atonement. The Lord said He would remember our sins "no more" (D&C 58:42). We may remember our sins, but we should do so with a sense of relief that they have been taken care of by Jesus. It's a waste of time and spiritual energy to constantly rehash the past and find reason to justify it. When a person has repented, confessed, and forsaken the sins of the past, it is time to move on. To dwell upon them is a sin of ingratitude. It is as if we are saying to Jesus, "Thanks for taking care of my sins, but I want to live in the Land of Regret and Misery and in some way suffer and self-atone and beat myself up for my poor choices." Only the devil would support that kind of thinking. We need to let go of the past. I've given the spiritual consequences of my past to Jesus. I've given those poor choices all of me they're ever going to have. I'm not going to give my todays and my tomorrows to my yesterdays.

CHAPTER SIXTEEN

Burying the Hatchet

Remember, the only constructive thing we can do with the past is to learn from it and to forgive others and ourselves. One man from my past, a wonderful young man I'll call Mark, came to me after meeting with his doctor. The doctor had told Mark that he had a venereal disease. Mark said, "Doctor, you don't understand, I couldn't. I just couldn't."

The doctor said, "Well, yes, young man, you most certainly do."

Mark was astounded. "It must be a mistake, you see, I was a virgin when I married my wife, and I'm a Mormon. I couldn't have a venereal disease."

The doctor replied, "So Mormons are immune from sexually transmitted diseases?"

Mark said, "Well, I couldn't."

So the doctor advised him, "If what you just said is true, I would go home and have a long talk with your wife because you don't get this from a toilet seat."

When Mark got home, he learned that his wife had been unfaithful, that she wasn't finished being unfaithful, and she wanted out of the relationship. This young man came to me wondering what to do. I told Mark that he would need to mourn the loss of "what should have been."

In grieving, we must go through certain stages before we get to the stage of acceptance. With a terminally ill patient, for example, the patient has to go through certain stages, they bargain with God, they feel anger, and they experience frustration at not being able to change something they wish did not exist. Working through certain stages is a very real part of grieving.

I said to him, "Mark, you have two beautiful children, and there is going to be life after the divorce. So you need to prepare for that."

Mark asked, "Then what do I do?" We talked on several different occasions, and he finally said, "I think I'm ready to forgive." The time required to forgive obviously varies with the spiritual preparation of each individual and his or her circumstances. It may take weeks, but it should not take years.

How long does it take to accept the death of loved ones? We may always miss them and be reminded of them on special days. To forgive doesn't mean we don't remember. It is how we choose to remember that matters. The pain of betrayal, the sting of death, or the remorse for past sins must all be laid at the feet of Jesus. I said to this young man, "If your wife had died crossing the plains, would you sit by her decaying body and wither away yourself, or would you take your two children and move on to the valley?"

He said, "I would move on to the Valley."

"What would you do with the body?"

"I would bury it, have a dedicatory prayer at the grave site, mark it with a head stone, and move on."

"Well, Mark, your marriage has spiritually died. Why don't you have a funeral for it, bury it, and move on with your life? All of your mourning, sorrow, and going back to relive the past to ponder how all of this might have been avoided if only you had been perfect will not bring it back to life."

After we mourn the loss of the relationship or "what should have been," there comes a deeper kind of acceptance, and perhaps a truer forgiveness. I suggested to this young man that he write a letter to his wife. Mark said that she wouldn't read it, that she'd be even angrier because she blamed him for all their problems anyway—"If I'd only been this, or if I had done that."

I explained to Mark that he wasn't going to *give* his wife the letter. I wanted Mark to write a letter to his wife about how betrayed he felt when he discovered her affair and that their temple covenants had been violated, and how he would have been willing to forgive her if she had been willing to be forgiven, and how devastating this was going to be for the two children. I wanted Mark to put the things he said to me about how his wife had destroyed his dream in the letter. The letter had to be honest, and he was to include every angry thought or feeling he possessed. "This isn't going to be a nice letter. Don't hold back. Your wife was unfaithful and still is. Tell her everything you would say, feel, or think if she were sitting in the chair right now. It may take you a couple of days to write the letter. When you have finished the letter, I want you to come back and read the letter to me."

When Mark returned, I had an empty chair in my office, and I had a large sign on the chair that had his wife's name. I had Mark face the empty chair with his knees against it. "For the next while, Mark, your wife is going to be in that chair, and I want you to read your letter to her just as if she were sitting there."

There was a tender spirit about his letter. It had been rewritten several times. Mark wept as he poured his heart out. The letter was several pages long. When he finished the letter he said as if to his wife, "There is a big part of me that still loves you, and I don't know what to do about it."

I told Mark that he wasn't done yet. "This is important, Mark. I want you to say very specifically, 'I forgive you for all the hurt, heartache, and sorrow you have caused me, and I turn you over to God. Let God judge between thee and me.' Turning her over to God is like going back to the temple altar and returning her to God. Mark, I need you to mean it when you say you will forgive her and turn her over to God. What you have done, Mark, is turn her over to Jesus. She is no longer your emotional or spiritual responsibility." I added, "A divorce is often more difficult than a death because the body isn't buried. The corpse is walking around, and you are going to have years of interaction with your wife because of those two children, but you have turned her over to Jesus." Mark did just that.

Then I pulled out an Indian hatchet and said, "Do you see this hatchet handle? Let me tell you about an old Indian tradition called, 'burying the hatchet.' When two warring factions wanted peace they would meet. They would take a tomahawk like this, and the two warring chiefs would put their marks on it. Then, the two patriarchs would go off and bury the hatchet by a cottonwood tree. However, they didn't forget where it was because the agreement was that once they buried the hatchet, they could never bring up that particular issue again. And if they ever wanted to discuss it again, they had to dig up the hatchet, bring it back to the person, and say, 'The peace is over. I can't forgive you.' It meant the war was on again."

I had Mark write the date he forgave his wife and turned her over to God on one side of another hatchet handle I had in my office. With a magic marker he wrote February 4, 1994. Then I asked him to put his and his wife's names on the other side of the hatchet handle, and I asked him if he was ready to bury the hatchet.

He said that he was. I asked him to choose a place that was important to him, somewhere he wanted to go to bury the hatchet. He said, "I want to go back to my mission field, to Peru."

I said, "Wow, that's a long way." He said, "I know. That's where I want it to be—a long, long way away." This young man climbed aboard an airplane, flew down to Peru, and when he got there, he climbed up a mountain where the wind was blowing and whistling. It was February 1994. He read the letter once more. He said, "I forgive you, and I turn you over to the Lord." Then he tore up the letter and let the wind carry it away. Next, he took the hatchet handle and buried it in a crevice high in the cliffs of the Andes.

When he came back I said, to him, "You will see your ex-wife for years to come. Whenever you feel tempted to go to the place of regret and depression, I want you to remember February 4, 1994, and a hatchet handle buried in a crevice in Peru and remember that you forgave her and turned her over to God. When you have occasion to think about it or think about her or the hurt, heartache, and sorrow, remember that you turned it over to the Lord on February 4, 1994, and that's His burden to carry from now on."

He came back from that experience with a positive attitude. A burden had been lifted off his shoulders. This man is not going to give his todays and his tomorrows to his yesterdays. He said, "When I came back, I saw her with a more loving attitude. I saw someone who needed help. I realized that it was not my stewardship or my responsibility to help her, but that I needed to be civil and kind. And so I had a cheerful disposition."

I talked with his wife after that. She said, "He must have not loved me very much if he's gotten over me so easily." That was her attitude. She couldn't believe he could be so positive and upbeat around her. She was desperately trying to find a reason to justify herself. She'll have to deal with that. But I get a card every year, usually in the middle of February, from this young man. "I was just thinking about February 4, 1994, and what a great burden was taken off my shoulders. I wanted to thank you for your part in that." My part in that was nothing, really, because we're talking about a principle of the gospel of Jesus Christ, the principle of forgiveness, and turning it over to the Lord, letting Him have that burden. Because if we live with resentment there is no room in our heart for love. Resentment devours love. We cannot look at someone, being filled with resentment, and find love at the same time. Those who have a contentious spirit are not allowed to participate in certain aspects of the endowment because their contentious spirit will drive the Spirit away for everyone else. It's important that we abide in the right spirit; the right spirit is to forgive.

Mark and others who have gone through this type of forgiveness experience also realize that to forgive doesn't mean we have to trust that person or that we have to like him or her. It certainly doesn't mean we have to be all huggy-kissy. We deal with them with respect and civility as discussed in chapter ten.

Letters of Mutual Forgiveness

Forgiveness letters can be an effective tool for healing and forgiveness in marriage. I recommend this forgiveness experience for all married couples, and it may need to occur more than once during the course of the marriage. Here is the procedure. The husband and wife each write a letter wherein they express the hurt, heartache, and sorrow their spouse has caused them. These letters are going to be read to their mate in my office or the two of them will go to a secluded place—a motel or someplace where they can be alone and not interrupted.

The content of the letter must be honest and express the depth of their feelings—the anger and betrayal the person truly feels. When they meet to read the letters they are to have stopped at the hardware store and picked up a hatchet handle. Whether they are in my office or alone, I have them sit in chairs facing one another knee to knee. I prefer a "ladies first" policy. The wife reads her letter to her husband. Under no circumstances is he to talk or interrupt once she begins to read the letter. His only responsibility is to listen carefully as she reads the letter.

The Apology

When she (let's call her Mary) has finished reading the letter, the husband (let's call him Bill) is going to apologize. Bill is going to specifically take responsibility for the hurt, heartache, and sorrow he has caused Mary. Remember, an apology is taking responsibility. An explanation or an attempt to answer with "why I did it" becomes an excuse. It transfers the responsibility for Bill's behavior to someone else, to some profound circumstance, some unique situation. None of Bill's explanations of his offenses, whatever they may be, will bring peace to the offended party. In fact, they will have the opposite effect. Why? Because what if that someone else comes back into Bill's life? Could not that "profound circumstance" reoccur? How about the "unique situation" repeating itself?

There is an unpopular point I insist upon. Don't ask, "why did you do X, Y, or Z?" As we mentioned earlier, there is only one true answer. "I had my free agency, and I am responsible for the choices I made. I was selfish and thoughtless. If I could go back and undo it I would. But there is no one to blame but myself. I have no excuse, and there is no profound circumstance or unique situation that caused me to do what I did. I am genuinely sorry."

Asking for Forgiveness

Back to Mary and Bill. When Mary has finished reading her letter, Bill looks into her eyes and, calling her by name, says, "Mary, will you forgive me for the hurt, heartache, and sorrow I have caused you?" He may even ask if he could hold her hand while he apologizes (that would be up to Mary; she may or may not be comfortable with this).

Mary calls him by name. "Bill, I forgive you for the hurt, heartache, and sorrow you have caused me."

It is very important that we call the person by name and that we say the words, "I forgive you." Obviously, people should not come to a forgiveness session unless they are ready and willing to forgive. As content communicators, we are going to hold each other accountable for our words.

Next, Bill reads his letter to Mary. She is to be silent and just listen as he reads the letter. When he has finished, Mary, calling her husband by name, says, "Bill, will you forgive me for the hurt, heartache, and sorrow I have caused you?"

The husband responds by calling her by name. "Mary, I forgive you for the hurt, heartache, and sorrow you have caused me."

These letters can be an effective tool for healing and forgiveness in marriage. If our mate decides to read his or her letter to us, we must then do our best to apologize. Let's say Bonnie and I do this. After Bonnie has read her eight pages and fifty-six items, I say, "Bonnie will you forgive me for the hurt, heartache, and sorrow I've caused you?"

She will say, "Yes, Johnnie, I forgive you."

Let's reverse it. Now I happen to write my letter of hurt, heartache and sorrow, and it fits on the back of a matchbook.

Bonnie says, "Johnnie, will you forgive me for any hurt, heartache, or sorrow I've caused you?"

What if I were to come back with "I don't know if I can. Few men have suffered as I've suffered. I'd like to, but I can't seem to be able to do it. I want to; I just can't." That is not real, and it is not right. So when Bonnie asks for my forgiveness, I am under a spiritual obligation to forgive and to turn it over to Jesus to judge. According to Mosiah 26:31, "Ye shall also forgive one another your trespasses; for verily I say unto you, he that forgiveth not his neighbor's trespasses when he says that he repents, the same hath brought himself under condemnation." We are to forgive when the person "says that he repents" not when we think he has repented. We are to give that person the benefit of the doubt and believe that his request for forgiveness is genuine. Ultimate sincerity is judged by the Lord. Doctrine and Covenants 64:10 states, "I, the Lord, will forgive whom I will forgive, but of you it is required to forgive all men." And so I say, "Bonnie, I forgive you." That is what forgiveness is about. We need to do that periodically so we don't harbor resentment.

It is now time for the husband and wife to bury the hatchet. They are to write their names and the date they forgave on the hatchet handle. It is important they go together to some remote spot and bury the hatchet. They remember where they put it. This symbolizes that these issues are now in the past. They cannot be talked about nor discussed again.

If one party or the other truly cannot let the issue alone, it is his or her responsibility to go and dig up the hatchet handle and bring it back to the husband or wife and express whatever unfinished business he or she has. At that point the spouse repeats the request for forgiveness. Calling the person by name, he or she asks, "Will you forgive me?" The person with the hatchet handle, the one who dug it up, is to say, "I forgive you." And it is their responsibility to rebury the hatchet, alone or together, it doesn't matter. What does matter is that the issues are not brought up again. In forty years I've only had two people I know of who went back and dug up the hatchet.

Remember, it's not a guarantee that the person is going to be perfect from that time forth. Forgiveness doesn't mean we have to trust the untrustworthy. It means we are going to forgive, we're going to treat the other with respect, and we are going to try to build a new history of positive behaviors with each other. We are not going to hold someone hostage to the past.

This is an important key to the principle of forgiveness. When I asked Bonnie to forgive me, she said she would, and she didn't ask for an explanation. She could have asked, as we often do, "Why did you do it?" But remember, there is only one answer to the why question. "I chose to do it. And I am not proud of myself. It was not a good thing. I made a bad decision. And I am the one responsible for that decision." Individual accountability in eternity is about me. It's about me accepting responsibility for what I do, for the choices I make.

My final counsel to all the Bills and Marys is not to become involved in the details of the transgression—the wheres and whens, and the specifics of the whats. It becomes brain clutter that will manifest itself in a thousand ugly future thoughts. You think you want to know the facts and the details. Without exception, the human female brain will constantly integrate those details into the future of the relationship, and the male brain will never fully recover once all the details are known. It is in the eternal best interests of both parties for the confession of details to be left with the bishop. For some women who read this, it may be too late, and they'll just have to live with the brain clutter and the insecurity it creates and try their best to deal with it. For those who have not yet crossed that bridge, don't. In all cases, after we have apologized and asked for forgiveness and buried the hatchet, we need to ask Heavenly Father to lift this burden from our shoulders. It will then be transferred appropriately to the Savior's shoulders, whose responsibility it is. He was foreordained for this stewardship before the foundations of the world (see 1 Peter 1:18–20). How much better we'd be if we could lay all our sorrows at Jesus' feet and move on with our lives. It is what He wants for us.

CHAPTER SEVENTEEN

Forgiving Ourselves

There are many of us that walk around trying, in some futile way, to pay for our own sins. We assume that if we suffer enough, we can prevent Christ from suffering for us. This, of course, is faulty thinking. There are two very important aspects of the Atonement, one of which is sacrifice and the other, suffering. We cannot carry out our own personal atonement as mortals. We may suffer later, but we will never qualify to make the sacrifice that Jesus made for us.

The Last Letter of Forgiveness Is to Ourselves

There are those who cannot seem to forgive themselves, even if the issues have been resolved with the bishop and the Lord. I ask them to write a letter to themselves. I tell them to write every stupid thing they've done, every disappointing decision, every wrong choice, every weakness that has afflicted them for years. This is a letter that may take a few days to write, and you'll need to keep to information safe from anyone's eyes. We must answer the question, "Why do I think I'm not worthy to enter the presence of God?" Imagine you are in a waiting room that looks like one of the celestial rooms in the temple. You are God's next appointment. In front of you is a pad and pen. You are to write down anything you've ever done from your earliest youth until this very moment on the pad. Whatever you write, you will not have to account for to God. What would you write? What dwells in your conscience that maybe only you and God know about? Write those things in your letter. What is it you regret? Write it down. In other words, bare your soul, get it all down in black and white. I had several pages when I did this.

Prop up a mirror in an empty chair. You need to be alone and not interrupted. Make arrangements so that this can happen. Sit in a chair opposite the chair with the propped-up mirror so that you are looking up close and personal at yourself. Read your letter out loud. "Here, John, this is what I find disappointing about decisions you've made in your life. This is where you have caused both of us a lot of hurt, heartache, and sorrow. Do you remember that nickel you took out of your grandmother's purse and went to the store and bought a candy bar? You were five, I think . . . Here are some really stupid things you did as a teenager." Everything—page after page. It was painful because I was being honest with myself.

When I was finished with the letter, I got down on my knees and asked God to forgive me, forgive me, and forgive me. Most of these things I had already dealt with, and I felt the Lord had forgiven me. But wait. I was still hanging on to remorse and regret. My conscience wasn't affecting me, but even after I had repented I was angry at myself for making poor choices. No matter how many times I talked to the bishop or asked the Lord to forgive me, there was a part of me that had not forgiven myself.

As you read this, if you feel there is some moral transgression or something that would keep you from having a temple recommend, I suggest you visit with your bishop about those matters. Even after you have that meeting with the bishop, the matter of forgiving yourself still remains.

Back to the empty chair with a mirror in it. So I got off my knees after reading my letter and asking God to forgive me, and I looked at my reflection in the mirror and said, "I forgive me. This day I forgive myself."

I had a hatchet handle I had purchased from the hardware store. With a magic marker I wrote my name and the date. I was the bishop at that time in Moscow, Idaho. I took the hatchet handle with my name and the date on it and drove toward Lewiston, Idaho, until I found a road and a sign I could remember. It was there I buried the hatchet. I made a promise to myself that I would not dwell on any of those negative thoughts about the past. And whenever I have occasion to think about any of those things, whatever they may be, I think these kinds of thoughts: *Thank goodness for the Atonement of Jesus Christ. Thank goodness that I can put those things behind me, and I can go forward, that I don't have to live in the land of regret and complaint.*

It is not the fact that we look back upon our sins; it is *how* we look back upon the past that matters. Our sins often have consequences that coexist with us. They're a part of our reality. But if we choose to look at our poor choices with a sense of gratitude for the Atonement, if we choose to look at the wonderful blessing of being forgiven, it does amazing things for us. Think of all the time people spend lamenting the past in their present. What if we traded our moments of regret and sorrow for a word of prayer, a prayer of gratitude for the Atonement, instead of a moment of regret? Maybe then we would not fall under the condemnation of a loving

Heavenly Father who has given us, through Jesus Christ, the gift of forgiveness, a gift we refuse to receive when we do not forgive ourselves and others.

Called to Love, Not Called to Judge

"Judge not unrighteously, that ye be not judged: but judge righteous judgment" (JST Matthew 7:2). There is a beautiful hymn by Eliza R. Snow entitled "Truth Reflects upon Our Senses." In the second verse are the words, "Jesus said, 'Be meek and lowly,' For 'tis high to be a judge" (*Hymns,* no. 273). Her poem was based upon Matthew 7:1–5. These words were spoken to the disciples. In the Church of Jesus Christ, there are only two job descriptions. One is to love and judge, and the other is to love. Judgment keys are strictly regulated. Jesus is the "Judge of [the] quick and [of the] dead" (Acts 10:42). John testified that Heavenly Father judges no man, but has "committed all judgment unto the Son" (John 5:22). Those judgment keys belong to anyone who has the authority to excommunicate a member of the Church. This means the keys of judgment are only given to General Authorities, stake presidents, and bishops. The bishop is referred to as a judge in Israel. These are they who are called to "love *and* judge." All other members of the Church are called upon to love. We are not called upon to pluck the mote from another's eye, but to give loving service.

Grandma Emma

One of the great regrets of my life is not being able to go back and love my Native-American grandmother. She was a perfect example of one who loved and never criticized. She ignored racial slurs. She simply didn't allow people to offend her. Her name was Emma. She was born on the Chehalis Indian Reservation and spoke English with a broken accent.

I was eleven months old when Pearl Harbor was attacked on December 7, 1941. With many others, my father joined the navy to redress the wrong of the "day that will live in infamy." My mother joined the work force, as many women did, to support the troops and to run the factories. She worked as a telephone operator all during the war. Many days she would work twelve hours.

As an only child I was cared for by day by my aunts and at night by my Indian grandmother. It was this wonderful woman who changed my diapers, washed me, fed me, and sang Indian lullabies to me when I cried. It was her golden-brown, oval face I would see until my mother came home. She called me "Jon-né." She would say, "Oh, Jon-né, it good to see [you]." Her words were choppy, her love was not. She was always glad to see her grandson. I was her first.

The war finally came to a close. Hitler was dead and the Japanese had signed an unconditional surrender on board the USS *Missouri,* the "Mighty Mo." All during those war years I remember my mother and grandmother saying, "When the war is over, your father will come home." I was six when I remember seeing my father for the first time. He was dressed in his navy blues with bell-bottom trousers and a collar with three white lines that went over his shoulders. He was wearing a white cap and spit-polished black shoes. Because there was a shortage of houses for all the returning servicemen, my father, mother, and I lived with my Indian grandmother. It took my father a year to remodel our future home before I left my Grandma Emma's place in Tumwater, Washington.

As I entered school and came in contact with the outside world I became aware that everyone didn't have an Indian grandma. I became judgmental and unloving. People made fun of the way she talked. My schoolmates would mock me and call me "Tonto." I found out that her first child, my Uncle Hank, was born out of wedlock. I learned that Grandmother Emma had divorced my grandfather. She also drank "firewater." (I told my children in later years that to be kissed by Grandma was an "intoxicating experience.")

My Indian grandmother really was a wonderful person. My mother said she never heard her speak ill of anyone, not ever. Frequently, my father would say, "Your grandmother misses you, son. She asks for you all the time. Let's go over and see her." But I was embarrassed by her. I judged her unworthy of my love. The five-mile trips became fewer and fewer between our place in Lacey and Grandma's in Tumwater. I stayed away. I was always "too busy" with football and friends. I made excuses and, finally, Dad stopped asking.

When I was nineteen, I was called on a mission to Mexico. I remember my father saying something about Grandma Emma's heart. Under duress, I went to see this loving and caring woman. When she saw me her whole countenance changed. "Oh, Jon-né, come, give hug." After a forever hug and an "intoxicating kiss," we sat and talked about my life. "Before [you] go, I give [you a] blessing." She took hold of both my hands and looked deep into my soul. Then she said ten things which I should have written down but didn't. I remember they all started with "May [you] always . . ." They had to do with the wind, the fire, the water, and the earth. I only recall the first one: "May [you] always walk with love in [your] heart."

One of the reasons I couldn't remember the rest of the blessing was because I had not always walked with love in my heart for this wonderful woman. She must have known that some people were embarrassed about her looking so much like the Indian she was, because she cut her hair and tried to look as much like others as she could. I only hoped in my heart of hearts that it was not me, and yet, before I left that day, I didn't just give her a hug, I clung to her and felt the sweet comfort of her love as I had in my childhood.

I left for my mission and received word she had died of a heart attack a couple of weeks after I was in Mexico. After the mission, I returned home, went to college, married, returned to the Northwest, and became interested in doing research in family history. I wasn't sure if Grandpa, who was a full-blooded Swede, wanted to be sealed to her or not. I determined they could work it out with God. My wife, Bonnie, acted as proxy for my grandmother and I for my "namesake" grandfather. What followed was a sacred experience wherein I knew they had accepted this work. I was dumbfounded. How could it be? She drank, she had a child out of wedlock, and her life was not exemplary. A scripture came to my mind. It was Mosiah 3:11: "And also his blood atoneth for the sins of those who have fallen by the transgression of Adam, who have died not knowing the will of God concerning them, or who have ignorantly sinned." I wept that I had been so judgmental of a grandmother who always loved her Jon-né.

By this time, my father had died in an auto accident, and Grandma Emma was survived by her illegitimate son, my Uncle Hank, who owned a tavern, and by her younger sister, Aunt Mildred. Everyone called her sister Millie. I traveled halfway across the state of Washington to the Yakama Indian Reservation, where Millie now lived. She was old and very wrinkled. Her eyes were bad. Except for my lighter skin, my father and I have the same build, as did my grandfather. We joked in the family that we were "bricks with ears." Because my father was born on March 28, when the small, purplish flower called a Johnny-Jump-Up was in bloom, his Indian name was Johnny-Jump-Up. If I ever wanted to get my father upset, all I had to say was "Jump-Up, Jump-Up." Then I would run for my life. He didn't want anyone calling him Jump-Up, but he couldn't keep his aunts and mother from calling him by that name.

Through her dim and aging eyes, my great-aunt Millie saw me and thought I was my father. She exclaimed, "Jump-Up! Is that you, Jump-Up?"

"No, Aunt Millie, it's son of Jump-Up."

She cried out, "Jon-né, oh, yes, Jon-né, son of Jump-Up. Come give me a big hug."

For a moment I was back in Grandma Emma's embrace. It was a bonding experience. I said to her, "Aunt Millie, I need you to tell me about my Grandma Emma. I have come because you are the only one who knows the truth of her life." Millie was silent for a moment, and then we spoke for two hours.

The first thing Aunt Millie said was, "She loved you, Jon-né. You light of life for her."

I had a lump in my throat and struggled to keep my emotions in control. "I know, Aunt Millie. I should have spent more time with her. Please tell me about her life."

Millie talked about life on the Chehalis Indian Reservation, where both she and Grandma Emma were born. She told me about Grandma Emma and how she loved to sing. I told Millie I remembered hearing her singing the Indian lullabies of my youth. We talked about a lot of things. Finally she told me that when Grandma Emma was a girl of fourteen years on the Chehalis Indian Reservation, a carload of boys had come in on the reservation and violated her. She had gotten pregnant as a result of that vile deed. She had chosen to keep the baby, and she gave birth to my Uncle Hank. She had started drinking alcohol because an Indian girl with a white man's child was not accepted on the Reservation. So at fifteen years of age, with her newborn baby, she moved to the nearby town of Elma, Washington. It was a rough logging town in 1909, but an Indian girl with a white baby was not accepted in Elma, Washington. She worked as a cook at a logging camp where she met and married my grandfather, a full-blooded Swedish logger who could barely speak English. I often wondered how the two of them, each with their thick accents, communicated with each other, but they did. My grandfather's name was Johannes, and everyone called him Johnny. Johnny Jump-Up, my father, was their firstborn. Four more children would follow. Grandma Emma never overcame the drinking habit that started when she was very young, very pregnant, rejected, and alone.

It was a five-and-a-half-hour drive from Yakima, Washington, to her grave in Tumwater, Washington. I could hardly see through my tears as I drove to the cemetery. At her grave I knelt and asked her to forgive me for having been so critical and judgmental of her. "For 'tis high to be a judge." This wonderful Indian Grandmother's only crime was loving a judgmental grandson. I have prayed many times for God to forgive me for the greater sin. She was guilty of drinking alcohol; I was guilty of denying her an association with a grandson who should have been loving and appreciative. I also denied myself an association with a loving, nonjudgmental Indian grandmother. Her every deed and act was loving. The words of her Indian blessing haunt me to this day. "May [you] always walk with love in [your] heart."

If I could go back, I would. I would stop by her house once a week and give her a big hug and kiss. I would ask her if I could run an errand for her or take her somewhere. If her lawn needed to be mowed, I would do it. But

I can't. I can't go back even though I stand on the same quiet earth. I'm confident she and the Lord have forgiven me. But it's still difficult to forgive myself for being judgmental, critical, and for not loving her the way I should have. As a grandson I was never called to judge. I was called to love, and I failed.

This experience has engraved itself upon my heart. I have tried to value all my relationships with family and friends and leave judgment with Jesus and with those who are called to "love and judge." As for me, I am simply called to "love." From that time on I made a special effort to stay in touch with both Aunt Millie and my Uncle Hank, the tavern owner.

One day I showed up at the back door of his tavern. A bartender opened the door and said, "What do you want?" My Uncle Hank knew that I had pretty much avoided him for most of his life. He probably saw me as a self-righteous, judgmental zealot and rightly so.

"Is my Uncle Hank here? I'd like to talk to him."

Leaning his head into the tavern, the bartender hollered, "Hey, Hank, there's some guy here that says he's your nephew."

My Uncle Hank came back. He looked a lot like my dad. Uncle Hank looked at me, but he was rather distant and cool. He said, "Yeah, what do you want?"

I said, "Hank, I'm sorry I haven't been a better nephew. You know, there are only three of us left in the family now. We are the only family that we have, and I am genuinely sorry that I haven't been a better nephew. I am here to try to be a better nephew, Hank, if you will have me."

This big, strong guy broke down and cried. Then he put his arm around me and gave me a hug. "I've always wanted to have a relationship with you. You know that I went to all of your football games—never missed a one. I was up there rootin' for you."

"I didn't know that, Uncle Hank, but thanks for being there for me."

Where are the Uncle Hanks, the Grandma Emmas in your life? They don't need our condemnation or our self-righteousness. Who might there be in the circle of our lives who need our love and forgiveness?

Why don't we take our love to our families and our frustrations to the Lord rather than profess love for God and take our judgments to our families? I have a testimony that as we take our love to our families that the Lord will intervene in the lives of our loved ones and soften hearts as he did Uncle Hank's. He will raise someone up to do something we cannot do in the lives of our loved ones. He will lead them and you; He will soften hearts and strengthen us. And sometimes, though it doesn't happen as often as we would like, He will remove a problem for us.

But we must reach out and make amends in these relationships that God will bring to our minds and hearts while there is still time on this side of the veil. We must pray that we will find a place to forgive and be able to truly let go of being judgmental. We are not called to judge; we are called to love.

The Alabaster Box

One of the greatest lessons in the scriptures is found in the story of the woman with the alabaster box. Now, in this alabaster box is one pound of spikenard, an herb worth a man's wages for three hundred days (see Matthew 26; Mark 14; Luke 7; John 12).

As Matthew tells it, Jesus was in Bethany at the house of Simon the leper. This was Simon the cured leper, because lepers were not allowed to live in the city unless they were cured. And while Jesus was at Simon's house, "there came unto him a woman having an alabaster box of very precious ointment, and poured it on his head, as he sat at meat. But when his disciples saw it, they had indignation, saying, To what purpose is this waste? For this ointment might have been sold for much, and given to the poor" (Matthew 26:7–9). When Jesus understood that they were upbraiding her, He told them to let her alone.

Mark adds a little bit more to the story. The Savior gently rebuked His disciples: "Why trouble ye her? she hath wrought a good work on me, For ye have the poor with you always, and whensoever ye will ye may do them good; but me ye have not always. She hath done what she could" (Mark 14:6–8).

We learn from John 12 that this woman was Mary, the sister of Martha and Lazarus. Through her act, she was accepting the fact that the Lord was going to die. What Mary was basically saying, as she was crying and washing His feet and drying them with her hair, was, "I accept you. I accept what you must do as my Redeemer and Savior." And while she was in the midst of these ministrations, Simon, who was Judas Iscariot's father, declared that she was wasting this costly ointment. And the Lord said, "Let her alone" (Mark 1:6). And then He added, "Wherefore I say unto thee, Her sins, which are many, are forgiven; for she loved much: but to whom little is forgiven, the same loveth little" (Luke 7:47).

The Final Judgment

The day will come when we will stand to be judged of Him. I will see my grandma Emma and my mother, my father, my wife, and my children, and I can see a long line of people waiting to testify of my shortcomings and weaknesses. And the Lord is going to say, "Does anyone have aught to say against Brother Lund here?" And as they line up, they will each have something valid to say. "Dad, you were this, and you weren't quite this. You put me outside on the porch when I was five years old because I wouldn't come to family prayer," and so on. And then there will come One who will say, after He's heard what He needs to hear, "Thank you all very much. Now, you let him alone, you let him alone. His sins, which are many, are forgiven him because he loved much." So may it be with each of us.

ABOUT THE AUTHOR

Dr. John L. Lund

John Lund is a well-known author and lecturer on relationships and communications. He has served for more than thirty years as a marriage and family counselor. He holds degrees in sociology and education from BYU, a second Master's degree in Educational Psychology from the University of Washington, and a PhD in Education from BYU. He is a popular speaker at Education Week. He and his wife, Bonnie, are the parents of eight children.